MICROECONOMICS

A Programmed Book

MICROECONOMICS
A Programmed Book

Third Edition

KEITH LUMSDEN
Stanford University

RICHARD ATTIYEH
University of California, La Jolla

GEORGE LELAND BACH
Stanford University

PRENTICE-HALL, INC., Englewood Cliffs, New Jersey

Library of Congress Cataloging in Publication Data

Lumsden, Keith.
    Microeconomics; a programmed book.

      1. Microeconomics—Programmed instruction.
I. Attiyeh, Richard, joint author.   II. Bach, George
Leland, joint author.   III. Title.
HB171.5.L84 1974   330'.07'7   74-1377
ISBN   0-13-581421-9

Printed In The United States of America

10   9   8   7   6   5   4   3

Prentice-Hall International, Inc., *London*
Prentice-Hall of Australia, Pty. Ltd., *Sydney*
Prentice-Hall of Canada, Ltd., *Toronto*
Prentice-Hall of India Private Ltd., *New Delhi*
Prentice-Hall of Japan, Inc., *Tokyo*

Contents

Preface

Our aim in writing this book and its companion piece *Macroeconomics* was to provide students, in a brief period of time, with a working knowledge of basic economics. It was our hope that these two books would prove a valuable tool as the primary reading material in courses that were of short duration (e.g., the one quarter course) or as introductory or supplementary material in more comprehensive courses. Both the reactions of instructors who have used the earlier editions and the results of a nationwide experiment* designed to evaluate their effectiveness lead us to believe that our objectives have been largely fulfilled. In a study involving 48 colleges and universities, students who read these books as supplementary material scored significantly higher than other students on the Test of Understanding College Economics. Furthermore, and of greater importance, students who spent 12 hours studying either of these books learned as much micro or macroeconomics as students who completed seven weeks on the same topics in a conventional course. On the basis of these results, we reached the following conclusion:

We feel that these results have important implications for the organization and teaching of the introductory course. Within the profession many believe that the introductory course should prepare a student to think in-

*See our paper "The Efficiency of Programmed Learning in Teaching Economics: The Results of a National Experiment," *American Economic Review,* LIX, No. 2 (May 1969), pp. 217-23.

telligently about major economic problems in modern society and that this goal can best be accomplished by teaching a few basic principles and applying them to a number of important problems. We are in agreement with this view. This study has shown that by using programmed learning materials the basic micro and macroeconomic theory can be taught in a relatively short period of time. Therefore more time can be devoted to teaching students how to apply the theory to social problems, both by going more deeply into the more important problems and by actually covering those topics scheduled for the end of the term that often fall victim to the school calendar. The use of these materials can have other advantages: First, the student can gain a good overview of the entire course at the very beginning, which helps him to put topics covered in the remainder of the course in meaningful perspective. Second, because a course taught in this manner emphasises the usefulness of economic theory in a problem-solving context, it promises a positive impact on the most important single factor in the learning process—namely, student attitude towards the subject.

Much of the increase in flexibility and teaching efficiency afforded by this text stems from its characteristics as a programmed book. A program is designed to develop complex ideas in small, carefully constructed steps. Each step, or frame, requires written responses focusing on key concepts, thereby ensuring continuous participation and involvement by the student. Furthermore, because the correct responses appear at the bottom of each page, it is possible for the student to see immediately whether he is grasping the material, thereby either reinforcing his interest or delineating areas that need further work. In this edition, to accommodate typical study patterns, the material has been divided into a larger number of shorter chapters. In addition, the brief tests appended to each chapter have been supplemented with detailed explanations of why the correct answers are correct and the wrong answers wrong.

Because of its analytical nature, economics lends itself well to the programming technique. Much of the material in both micro and macroeconomics can be usefully broken down into frames that have desired responses that are both basic and unambiguous. In this text, we analyze the way a market system will lead to an efficient allocation of resources. In studying the efficiency of such an economic system, situations in which resources will not be efficiently allocated through the market mechanisms are examined. Although this edition has been expanded to include imperfect competition, most of our attention is directed toward the operation of a perfectly competitive system. Because the text is intended to give the reader a thorough grounding in basic microeconomic theory, considerable attention is paid to the basic analytical tools, including a new chapter on diagrammatic exposition. In this edition, we have incorporated many of the suggestions made by instructors and students, as well as alterations indicated by detailed data from our study. For example, in response to suggestions from many instructors we have added a chapter on income distribution.

We are extremely grateful to Cheryl Smith and Michael E. Melody of Prentice-Hall, Inc., for their assistance in preparing the book for publication.

Keith Lumsden
Richard Attiyeh
George Leland Bach

1

Introduction: The Nature of Economic Problems

Why study economics?

Why has society been willing to pay Jack Nicklaus over $1 million just to play golf?

People say we have a shortage of hospitals and doctors but an excess of pornography and drugs. Is this true?

Why is the price of something essential like water so low when the price of something frivolous like diamonds is so high?

Why do we subsidize students at universities who will, on the average, earn high incomes during their working lives?

Why do minority-group members and white females, on the average, receive lower wages than do white males?

If you prefer logical, rather than emotional, responses to these questions, you will find it profitable to study economics. We will find it profitable if you choose this book in your pursuit of knowledge.

Make sure that you fill in the blanks, or delete the wrong responses in blanks where you are given a choice, before comparing your responses with those at the bottom of the page. Reading the book in this way should ensure that you will learn as much microeconomic theory as a fellow student after seven weeks of a typical course. This is your incentive to choose this book over others.

In a programmed text, we proceed from the simple to the complex. Our first example is, therefore, simple, but enlightening.

1.1

Suppose your father, wishing to encourage you to study more, made the following proposition: For every point of your grade point average (GPA) this term he will pay you $4 per day. If your GPA is 2.0, you will receive $8 per day. If an A is equivalent to 4 points, a B, 3 points, a C, 2 points, and a D, 1 point, an A average would be worth $ _____ per day. Two B's and two C's would be a _(2.5/2.0/1.5)_ GPA and, therefore, would be worth only

$ _____ per day.

1.2

You realize immediately that the higher your grades, the _(higher/lower)_ your income from your father. Because more time devoted to studying means higher grades, the way to increase your income from your father is to spend _(more/less)_ time studying.

1.3

The more time you spend studying, however, the _____ time you have left for other income-earning pursuits, such as waiting on tables, baby-sitting, or pumping gas.

1.4

Your father surmised that the reason your GPA fell last semester was that you took outside jobs to earn income. He realized that in order to earn such income, you were devoting _____ to outside jobs that could otherwise have been spent studying.

1.5

Thus, your father's proposition is really an attempt to encourage you to spend

_____ time studying and _____ time on outside jobs.

Answers

1. 16 · 2.5 · 10
2. higher · more
3. less
4. time
5. more · less

1.6

The more time spent on outside employment, the _____ your income from outside sources. However, the more time spent on outside employment, the less time available for study, and the _____ your GPA.

Therefore, the more time spent on outside employment, the _____ your income from your father.

1.7

Suppose each day, on the average, you have six hours that are uncommitted to sleeping, eating, going to class, and pure entertainment. You have _____ hours per day that may be used to earn _____ by studying or from outside employment.

1.8

You know that income from your father depends upon your _____, which in turn depends upon the _____ you spend studying.

1.9

Income from outside employment depends upon the hourly wage paid and the number of _____ you are employed.

1.10

Because you have six hours to allocate each day, your total daily _____ will be composed of GPA income from your father and/or wage income from outside employment. The more hours per day you devote to outside employment, the _____ your income from that source, but the _____ the number of hours available for study.

Answers

   6. higher · lower · lower
   7. six · income
   8. GPA · time
   9. hours
  10. income · greater · smaller

1.11

The smaller the number of hours devoted to study, the _____ your

GPA, and the _____ your income from your father.

1.12

Thus, an increase in income from outside employment means a(n) _____
in income from your father.

1.13

In other words, there is a cost associated with earning income from an outside
job that is over and above the work effort involved. This cost is the income that

you could have earned by spending that time _____ . Economists
call this *opportunity cost.*

1.14

When you are forced to choose from alternatives, you must give up one thing to

get another. What you give up is the _____ cost of what you get.

There is an opportunity _____ in taking an outside job because it is
necessary to take time away from something else. It is impossible, given that you
have only six hours to study and/or work, to increase time spent working with-

out _____ the time spent studying.

1.15

Likewise, in this example, it is impossible to increase income from outside

employment without _____ income from your father. This loss of

income from your father is the _____ cost of the outside income
you earn.

Answers

11. lower · lower
12. decrease
13. studying
14. opportunity · cost · decreasing
15. decreasing · opportunity

1.16

What your father hopes to accomplish from his proposal is a(n) _____

in hours devoted to studying and a(n) _____ in hours devoted to

outside jobs. He hopes to do this by raising the _____ _____
of the outside income you can earn.

1.17

Suppose your aim is to earn as high a daily income as possible, either from
studying or outside employment or a combination of both. What would you do?

a. Spend six hours studying.
b. Spend six hours working.
c. I do not have enough information to answer the question. *(a/b/c)*   .

1.18

Quite correct, you do not yet have enough information. Some of the information necessary to answer the question is how your GPA changes as you vary the
time spent studying. Suppose we agree on the relationship shown in Table 1.1:

Table 1.1

STUDY TIME AND GPA

Average hours spent studying per day	GPA
6	4.00
5	3.75
4	3.33
3	2.75
2	2.00
1	1.08
0	0.00

Answers

16. increase · decrease · opportunity cost
17. c

If you devoted all your uncommitted hours to studying, you would, on the average, study six hours per day; your resultant GPA would be 4.00, and at $4

per point your father would pay you $ _____ per day. In this case,

your income from outside employment would be $ _____. Your

total daily income therefore would be $ _____.

1.19
Remember, your goal is to earn the highest possible daily _____
from both sources combined. Do you now have enough information to decide
how to allocate your six hours to achieve this end? _(yes/no)_

1.20
If you devoted five hours to studying, your GPA would be _____.
Because your father pays you $4 per point, your income from him would be

$ _____.

1.21
Now, five hours devoted to studying leaves _____ hour(s) free for
outside employment. If you can earn only $0.50 per hour on outside employ-
ment, your five hours studying plus one hour on the outside will give you a total

income of $ _____ + $ _____, which equals

$ _____.

1.22
This solution is clearly _____ satisfactory to you, compared with study-

ing six hours per day, because your total income is now _____ than
before.

Answers
  18.   16 · 0 · 16
  19.   income · no
  20.   3.75 · 15
  21.   1 · 15 · .50 · 15.50
  22.   less · lower

1.23

If, however, your outside employment paid $2 per hour, your five hours study-
ing plus one hour working outside would yield a total income of

$ _____, which is higher than the $ _____ from
studying six hours per day.

1.24

Thus, given that your aim is to maximize (make as large as possible) your daily
income, there are several things you must know before deciding how to allocate

your six hours per day. First, you must know how much _____ you

can earn from your father by studying for different amounts of _____.

Second, you must know how much _____ you can earn by spending
different amounts of time working at outside jobs.

1.25

The same kind of calculation is made, consciously or subconsciously, when you
decide to spend the evening studying in the library or going out on a date. You
cannot easily quantify in dollars "the library" versus "a date," but somehow you
make the decision. When you feel studying in the library is worth more to you
(in "psychic income") than going out on a date, you go to the library. Similarly,

in this example, where you are trying to maximize _____, when you
can earn more income by switching a study hour to outside employment, you
(should/should not) make that switch.

1.26

This simple problem, concerned with the best way to allocate your six hours,
is really an economic problem. Economics is concerned with the best way to
allocate *scarce resources* among various alternative uses to make some
individual or group as well off as possible. In our simple example, the scarce
resource to be allocated is _(time/income)_ . The alternative uses of your

time are outside work and _____, and you are as well off as

possible when your daily _____ is maximized.

Answers

23.   17 · 16
24.   income · time · income
25.   income · should
26.   time · studying · income

1.27

When economists think about the economy as a whole, the scarce resources are all those things that help produce the goods and services we want. Roads,

machine tools, schoolteachers, and farmland are examples of _____ resources.

1.28

Some of the alternatives society faces are more schools or more hospitals, more butter or more guns, more pop records or more classical records. Just as in our simple example income from outside work has an opportunity cost of income

from your father, so in the real world there are _____ costs. In order to produce more of one good, let us say, spaghetti, it is necessary to give

up some amount of other goods. This latter amount, of course, is the _____ _____ of the extra spaghetti.

1.29

We do not have enough _____ to produce all the goods and services everyone wants. It is for this reason that we must choose what to produce, and

it is for this same reason that we say the economy's resources are _____.

1.30

Because resources are _____ , we cannot have everything we want. Consequently, as a nation we are faced with the economic problem of deciding

how to use our _____ _____ .

1.31

Before we try to use economic analysis to understand our complex economy, let us try to master our simple example. That is, before you try to comprehend

how society can use its _____ _____ to its best advantage, let us solve the economic problem of how to use your scarce resource,

which is _____ , to maximize your daily _____ .

Answers

27. scarce
28. opportunity · opportunity cost
29. resources · scarce
30. scarce · scarce resources
31. scarce resources · time · income

1.32

From the information you already have, it is possible to construct a table of figures that will permit you to see the best allocation of working time. This is the allocation that __(minimizes/maximizes)__ your daily income. Assume the hourly wage from outside employment is $2 per hour.

1.33

Table 1.2, showing the relevant information, is incomplete. Fill in the blanks. To do so, you will need to remember that your father is willing to pay to you

$ _____ daily per each point of your GPA.

Table 1.2

TIME ALLOCATION AND INCOME

Hours spent in			Daily income		
Employment (1)	Studying (2)	GPA (3)	Employment (4)	Father (5)	Total (6)
0	6	4.00	$ 0	$16	$16
1	5	3.75	2	15	17
2	4	3.33	4	a) _____	b) _____
3	3	2.75	6	c) _____	d) _____
4	2	2.00	8	8	16
5	1	1.08	10	4.32	14.32
6	0	0.00	12	0	12

1.34

From Table 1.2, it is possible to determine the allocation of time that maximizes your income. This allocation is _____ hours spent studying and _____ hours in employment. In this way, you can earn a total of _____ per day.

1.35

By looking at this allocation problem in a slightly different way, it is possible to develop an analytical tool that is very useful in dealing with more difficult economic problems. As we saw above, an allocation problem concerns the use

of some _____ resource so as to _____ something.

1.36

For the economy as a whole, we would be concerned about how to use the

nation's _____supply of land, labor, and capital (its resources) to

_____ social welfare. In our simple example, you must decide how

to use your limited _____ to maximize your daily _____ .

1.37

We solved your allocation problem by calculating for every possible allocation of six hours the resulting total income and by choosing the allocation with the

_____ total income.

1.38

An alternative way to look at the problem is to start with a particular allocation, say five hours studying and one hour working, and to determine how total income changes as you change the allocation of time. If there is some way to change the allocation to increase total income, then you ___(should/should not)___ make the change. If there is no change that will increase total income, then you

must already have the _____ of time that gives the _____ total income.

1.39

Let us find out what happens when you reallocate one hour of your study time to outside employment. Beginning with a five hour study/one hour work combination, from Table 1.2 you can see that an increase in one hour of study time

would raise your GPA from _____ to _____ . Corre-

Answers

35. scarce · maximize
36. scarce · maximize · time · income
37. maximum
38. should · allocation · maximum
39. 3.75 · 4.00

spondingly, the income you receive from your father would rise from $ _____

to $ _____ .

1.40

That is, starting from a level of study of five hours per day, an increase in study-

ing of one hour per day adds $ _____ in income from your father.
This, of course, is the difference between an income of $16 per day associated

with a GPA of _____ and an income of $ _____
associated with a GPA of 3.75.

1.41

The increase in studying time must come from an equal _____ in
time spent working. Consequently, your income from outside employment

would fall from $2 to $ _____ . Your new total income in this case

would be $ _____ , which would be _____ than its
initial level.

1.42

Carefully trace what is happening. Adding one study hour from five to six hours

per day would increase your GPA; it also would _____ the daily

income from your father by $ _____ . The accompanying decrease
of one working hour would reduce daily income from outside employment by

$ _____ . This latter amount is the opportunity _____
of the extra income from your father.

1.43

Would you increase your total income by making this change? ___(yes/no)___

Essentially, you would give up $ _____ of income from working

in return for $ _____ of income from studying, which is a net
___(gain/loss)___ of $1. In other words your total income would
___(increase/decrease)___ by the amount of $ _____ .

Answers
  39.   15 · 16
  40.   1 · 4.00 · 15
  41.   decrease · 0 · 16 · lower
  42.   increase · 1 · 2 · cost
  43.   no · 2 · 1 · loss · decrease · 1

For your convenience, Table 1.2 is reproduced here.

Table 1.2

TIME ALLOCATION AND INCOME

Hours spent in			Daily income		
Employment (1)	Studying (2)	GPA (3)	Employment (4)	Father (5)	Total (6)
0	6	4.00	$ 0	$16	$16
1	5	3.75	2	15	17
2	4	3.33	4	13.32	17.32
3	3	2.75	6	11	17
4	2	2.00	8	8	16
5	1	1.08	10	4.32	14.32
6	0	0.00	12	0	12

1.44

Clearly, it ___(would/would not)___ pay to change a 5-1 study-work combination to 6-0. But what about a change in the other direction? From Table 1.2, you can

see that a decrease in study time to four hours would mean a _____ in your GPA from 3.75 to 3.33 and a decrease in income from your father of

$ _____ .

1.45

Even though this change reduces income from your father by $1.68, it would still be worth making if the hour saved from studying could by used to earn

more than $ _____ from outside employment. Because you can earn $2 per hour by working, the change from a 5-1 study-work allocation to

4-2 would _____ your total income by $ _____ .

1.46

In this case, the $ _____ you lose from your father by studying one

hour less is more than made up for by the $ _____ you can earn by using that hour working on an outside job.

Answers

44. would not · decrease · 1.68
45. 1.68 · increase · 0.32
46. 1.68 · 2

1.47

Thus, it is clear that the change from 5-1 study-work allocation to 4-2 is worth making. Does this, by itself, necessarily mean that the 4-2 combination is best? __(yes/no)__ In principle, it is possible that further changes in the direction of less study and more work would lead to further increase in total _____ .

1.48

Consider the possibility of changing to a 3-3 study-work combination. The decline in study from four to three hours would lead to a __(gain/loss)__ in income from your father amounting to $ _____ , while the extra hour worked would increase your outside income by _____ .

1.49

In this case, because the __(gain/loss)__ in income from your father is not matched by the _____ in outside income, the change __(is/is not)__ worth making.

1.50

You have seen that a change from the 4-2 study-work combination to either 5-1 or 3-3 _____ your total income. Therefore, the 4-2 study-work combination must yield the _____ total income.

1.51

What we have seen is that whether you consider this problem by looking at the total income earned from alternative allocations or by considering changes in income from _____ in allocation you arrive at the same solution. This is true because at a point of maximum income a change in any direction will _____ income.

Answers

47. no · income
48. loss · 2.32 · 2
49. loss · gain · is not
50. decreases · maximum
51. changes · reduce

1.52

Economists call the approach that concentrates on changes in allocations

marginal analysis. When using _____ analysis, you consider things
at the margin rather than looking at the total.

1.53

In our example, we could say that a shift from 3-3 study-work combination to

4-2 would yield an increase in income from your father of $ _____ ,
which is the *marginal benefit* of this change. We could say that the accompany-

ing loss in outside income of $ _____ is the *marginal cost* of the
change.

1.54

In shifting from a 3-3 study-work combination to 4-2, because the _____

benefit exceeds the _____ cost, the change ___*(is/is not)*___
worth making.

1.55

When you increase your study time, there are both benefits and costs because
your time is scarce. Because time is scarce, you cannot increase study time with-

out taking _____ away from some other use. As a result, you not

only receive the marginal _____ of increased income from your

father by studying more but you also must bear the marginal _____
of decreased income from outside employment.

1.56

Generalizing from this example, we can establish several important economic
principles: First, it is necessary to make choices whenever resources (for exam-

ple, time) are _____ .

Answers

52. marginal
53. 2.32 · 2
54. marginal · marginal · is
55. time · benefit · cost
56. scarce

1.57
Second, whenever a choice must be made there is an opportunity _____
involved. When you choose an apple over an orange, the orange is the _____
_____ of the apple.

1.58
Third, however your resources are allocated to begin with, when you consider a
change in that allocation there are both a marginal _____ and a
marginal _____ .

1.59
Finally, a change is worth making only when the _____ _____
is greater than the _____ _____.

1.60
These facts of economic life hold true whether we consider your simple
problem of allocating your time or the complex problem of allocating the

economy's many _____ resources.

1.61
The war in Vietnam provides a case in point. To carry out this war, it was

necessary to use substantial quantities of the nation's _____ _____ .
Sadly, one great cost incurred was the substantial loss of human life—a loss that
cannot be measured solely in economic terms.

1.62
Over and above this tragic loss of life, there was also an additional, enormous
opportunity cost. In 1971, it was estimated that up until then the cost of the
war to the United States, excluding human casualties, had exceeded $100

Answers
57. cost · opportunity cost
58. benefit (cost) · cost (benefit)
59. marginal benefit · marginal cost
60. scarce
61. scarce resources

billion. If the war had been avoided, the resources used to carry out the war
___(could/could not)___   have been used to produce civilian commodities that
American families and businesses could have put to good use. If there had been
no war, the land, labor, and capital used to produce jet fighters, napalm, and
mortars ___(could/could not)___   have been used to produce new schools, better

health services, and more clothing. Some facts will illustrate the _____
cost of the war; that is, alternatives foregone when scarce resources were devoted to the war effort.

1.63
Roughly half of all U.S. families could now have a private swimming pool or

another automobile if the scarce _____ used to carry out the war
had been diverted to the swimming pool or automobile industries over the
span of the war.

1.64
In fiscal year 1969, the year of peak expenditures for Vietnam, it was estimated
that of the $28.8 billion of military expenditures in Vietnam, $7.3 billion
would have been spent for defense in the absence of that war. Thus, the differ-

ence of $ _____ billion represents the extra (or marginal) cost of
the war itself for that year. If this amount were given to the 10 million poorest
families instead of being spent in Vietnam, these families could have received
additional income of over $2,000 per family in 1969. Doing without a signifi-
cant lessening of poverty in the U. S., therefore, can be considered one measure of

the _____ cost of the war. As you will see later in the text, exact
definitions of the extent of poverty, its causes and cures, pose many problems
for our society. What is obvious, however, given limited resources, is that more

of one type of good means _____ of some other goods.

1.65
The Vietnam war versus no Vietnam war is the classic choice between "guns
and butter." In deciding to expand the war, the government chose to reallocate

Answers

62. could · could · opportunity
63. resources
64. 21.5 · opportunity · less

resources to produce _____ guns and _____ butter.
The political and strategic gain resulting from more "guns" is the marginal

_____ .

1.66
Those who supported the government's Vietnam policy obviously believed that

the war's marginal _____ outweighed its marginal _____ .

1.67
Those who opposed the war held the opposite view. To them, reallocating
resources from fighting, let us say, poverty in the United States to fighting

communism in Vietnam _(increased/decreased)_ the welfare of the American
people.

1.68
Another example in which the concepts of scarcity, opportunity cost, and marginal analysis are useful is the battle over the California redwood forests.
Redwood trees make both beautiful forests and handsome lumber. Unfortunately, if you cut a forest for lumber, it is _(just as/no longer)_ beautiful to
look at. Furthermore, there are not enough redwoods to fully satisfy people's
desires for both beautiful forests and handsome lumber. If society chooses to
preserve a forest rather than use the wood for lumber, the foregone lumber is

the _____ _____ of the beautiful forest.

1.69
In economic terms, then, we have said that redwoods are a natural resource that

is _____ and for which there are alternative uses. Consequently,

for every grove of redwoods, we _(have no/must make a)_ choice.

Answers
65. more · less · benefit
66. benefit · cost
67. decreased
68. no longer · opportunity cost
69. scarce · must make a

1.70

Whichever choice is made, we must give up one of the alternatives. That is, we

will have to accept the _____ cost. If we choose to cut a grove,
we must face up to the loss of a beautiful forest.

1.71

It will pay to cut the grove, however, only if the marginal _____ of

the extra lumber outweighs the marginal _____ of one less redwood
grove.

1.72

In these examples, we have shown how an economist analyzes social problems.
But one rather obvious point should have been made explicit. Before you can
compare the marginal benefit and marginal cost of any change, you must know

what the marginal _____ and marginal _____ are. In
both of the policy problems discussed, it was necessary to make subjective
value judgments before you could make any decision. That is, you had to sub-

jectively weigh the _____ benefits of the war, for instance,
against the marginal costs. Much bitter strife on college campuses and in cities
over the war issue is evidence that different groups of people hold widely
different value judgments on these benefits and costs.

1.73

In all economic problems, you must know people's preferences as well as their

alternatives before you can make a rational decision. Economics _(can/cannot)_
determine value judgments, but once society's preferences and available resources are known, the application of economic principles will lead to rational
decision making.

Answers

 70. marginal
 71. benefit · cost
 72. benefit · cost · marginal
 73. cannot

REVIEW QUESTIONS

Below each question is a suggested explanation of the correct answer. Before
reading the explanation, circle the response you believe is correct. Make sure
you read through all the responses and know why one is correct and the others
are incorrect before making your decision.

1.1

This question is based on the following statement:
    "The question facing our government is whether to build a new highway
system or establish public libraries throughout the country during the next
three years. Resources for both projects are not available. It must be one or the
other."
    The opportunity cost of the new highway system mentioned in the paragraph
above is

a. greater than the economy can afford.
b. national libraries.
c. the money required to pay for it.
d. the resources required to build it.

If the government were to build the new highway system, it would have to
raise the money to pay for it, and resources would be required to build it.
But neither of these costs is the opportunity cost of the highway system.
Whether the government builds a highway system or establishes public libraries, the money will be spent and the resources used. The opportunity cost of
a good is the alternative that must be given up to obtain that good. Whether
the opportunity cost of the new highway system is greater than the economy
can afford depends on whether it will yield lower benefits than the library
system. If it does, the opportunity cost is too high, and the highway system
should not be built. The correct response is b.

1.2

What is meant by the assertion that every economic system, be it communist,
socialist, or capitalist, faces the fundamental fact of scarcity?

a. As a country starts to develop, many commodities that were scarce be-
    come more plentiful, and people become better off on the average.

b. When jobs are unavailable, many low skilled, poorly paid workers, including a disproportionate number of minority workers, become poverty stricken.
c. Insufficient resources exist to satisfy all the wants in any given society.
d. All economies allocate too many resources to private consumption and too few to public goods.

Although a, b, and d are all true and although they are all concerned with scarcity, none of them explains the fundamental fact of scarcity faced by each and every nation in the world today. This scarcity arises because no matter what the resources any nation in the world has today, they are insufficient to satisfy all the wants of the people of that nation. The correct response is c.

1.3
Economic resources are termed *scarce resources* because they

a. are not available in sufficient quantities to meet all orders for them.
b. are not available in sufficient quantities to meet all wants for them.
c. cannot be increased in quantity to any significant extent.
d. are of primary importance in satisfying the needs of society.

A resource is scarce whenever having more of it would make someone better off. It is possible for a resource to be scarce even though enough is available to fill all orders (people might like to have more cars but cannot afford to buy more). A resource that cannot be increased in quantity may be scarce, but so may resources that can be. Whenever there are unsatisfied wants, resources are scarce. The correct response is b.

1.4
"Because resources are scarce, it is necessary for our society to economize." Which, if any, of the following does this statement imply should be done?

1. Consumers should save more.
2. The government should reduce its expenditure for goods and services.
3. The production of luxuries should be reduced.

a. 1 and 2 only
b. 2 and 3 only
c. 1 and 3 only
d. None of the above

The basic economic problem facing each nation is how to make the best possible use of its scarce productive resources. Neither consumers saving more, reducing government expenditure, nor reducing the production of luxuries implies economizing in this sense. The most efficient use of resources could, in some circumstances, involve less saving, increasing government expenditure, or increasing the production of luxuries. The best use of resources will involve the production of the combination of resources that satisfies people's wants as fully as possible. The correct response is d.

2

Marginal Analysis

2.1

In Chapter 1, you learned that whenever resources are _____ a choice must be made among the alternative uses of those resources. Because resources are scarce, whenever they are put to one use there will be the

_____ cost of the benefit that would have resulted had they been put to an alternative use.

2.2

For example, as was discussed in Chapter 1, to carry out the Vietnam war it was necessary to use _____ that could have been used to satisfy domestic wants. That is, the civilian commodities that could have been produced with the resources used to fight the Vietnam war were the

_____ cost of the war.

Answers

    1. scarce · opportunity
    2. resources · opportunity

2.3

This can be seen in terms of Table 2.1 and Figure 2.1, which illustrate in terms of "guns" and "butter" the alternative combinations of military and civilian

output that could have been produced with society's _____ in some given time period.

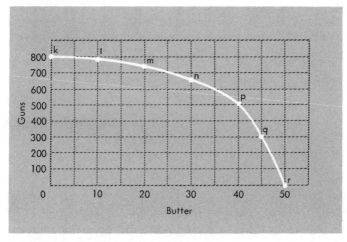

FIGURE 2.1   Production possibilities curve

Table 2.1

PRODUCTION ALTERNATIVES

Guns	Butter (Tons)
800	0
780	10
730	20
660	30
500	40
300	45
0	50

2.4

If all resources were devoted to the production of guns, we would be able to

produce _____ guns and nothing else. We would be at point

_____ on the production possibilities curve.

Answers

   3.   resources

   4.   800 · k

2.5
Now, if a small amount of resources were devoted to the production of butter,

as at the point 1, we would be giving up _____ guns to obtain

_____ tons of butter.

2.6
The point q represents _____ guns and _____ tons of

butter. By moving from k to q, therefore, we would be giving up _____

guns to obtain _____ tons of butter.

2.7
Is it worth moving from k to q? _(yes/no/don't know)_

2.8
The reason we do not know if it is worth moving from k to q is because we do
not know how society values guns versus butter. We do not know, for this

society, in moving from k to q, whether the benefit of _____
more tons of butter is worth the cost of _____ fewer guns.

2.9
This example is similiar to all resource allocation problems in economics. What
proportion of resources should be allocated to the production of different

goods? The _____ _____ curve tells what outputs of
each good will be associated with different resource allocations. The economic
problem is: Which of the different combinations of goods that can be pro-

duced with society's limited _____ should be produced?

2.10
How to allocate scarce resources to make society as well off as possible is the

_____ problem.

Answers
5. 20 · 10
6. 300 · 45 · 500 · 45
7. don't know
8. 45 · 500
9. production possibilities · resources
10. economic

2.11

To understand the economic problem of choice from among alternative resource allocations, let us consider again our simple work-study example from Chapter 1. You will recall that the objective was to maximize the

_____ you could earn by allocating your time between work and

study. In this example, your scarce resource was _____ .

2.12

The alternative feasible combinations of work and study time can be seen in Table 2.2 and Figure 2.2

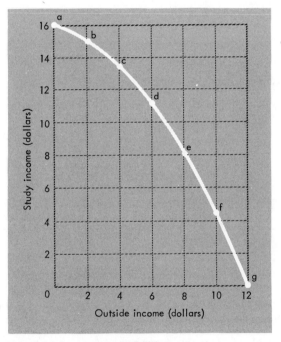

FIGURE 2.2   Income possibilities curve

The points a, b, c, d, e, f, and g represent the different combinations of study

income plus outside income obtainable by using the _____ hours available, that is, by using the amount of the scarce resource available.

Answers

   11. income · time

   12. 6

Table 2.2

INCOME ALTERNATIVES

	Study		Outside Work	
Hrs.	Income	Hrs.	Income	
6	$16	0	$ 0	
5	15	1	2	
4	13.32	2	4	
3	11	3	6	
2	8	4	8	
1	4.32	5	10	
0	0	6	12	

2.13

Point a, for instance, represents study income of $ _____ and out-

side income of $ _____ . This combination of income is obtained

from _____ hours of studying and _____ hours of
outside work.

2.14

Point d represents study income of $ _____ and work income of

$ _____ . This point corresponds to _____ hours

of studying and _____ hours of outside work.

2.15

If we took all possible study-work combinations, we would obtain a smooth
curve connecting points a through g, as in Figure 2.2. For instance, 5½ hours of

outside work would yield an outside income of $ _____ , and ½
hour of studying would yield a study income greater than zero but less than

the $ _____ that could be obtained from one hour of studying.
The point so derived would lie on the curve in Figure 2.2 between the points

_____ and _____ .

Answers

    13. 16 · 0 · 6 · 0
    14. 11 · 6 · 3 · 3
    15. 11 · 4.32 · f · g

2.16

The curve in Figure 2.2, then, is the income possibilities curve that gives all the

alternative combinations of work and study _____ that are possible
to attain with the six hours available to you. The economic problem, of course,

is to pick the allocation of time that yields the _____ income.

2.17

In this simple case, it is possible to find the best allocation of time by considering all possible allocations of time. In more complex situations, for example
allocating resources for the entire economy, such a straightforward approach
is not possible. For that reason, it will be useful to consider in detail the marginal
approach that was developed in Chapter 1. You will recall that given any
initial situation you can imagine allocating one unit more of your resources
to some particular use. This change will involve a benefit, which is called the

(total/marginal) _____ benefit, and a cost, which is the _____ cost.

2.18

In our example, we can imagine allocating one more unit of time (an hour) to
studying. The extra income from your father as a reward for the ensuing

higher grade point average is the _____ _____ of
studying. But because you can study more only by working less, there is an
opportunity cost involved. The income you give up by working one hour less

is the marginal _____ of studying.

2.19

It is helpful to analyze these concepts with the help of diagrams. Look at
Figure 2.3. Along the horizontal axis, we measure the hours worked in outside
employment, and along the vertical axis we measure the hourly _____

_____ that can be earned from outside employment.

Answers

    16.   income · maximum
    17.   marginal · marginal
    18.   marginal benefit · cost
    19.   wage rate

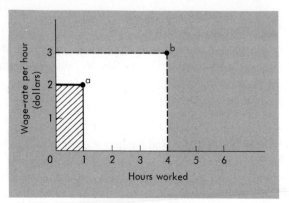

FIGURE 2.3   Income from outside employment depending on hours
worked and the wage rate

2.20
Two points are plotted in Figure 2.3. Each point represents a particular combination of hours worked and wage rate. Point a stands for one hour worked at a

wage rate of $ _____ per hour. Point b represents _____

hours worked at a wage rate of $ _____ per hour.

2.21
If you worked one hour per day at a wage rate of $2 per hour, your daily

income would be $ _____ . In Figure 2.3, this is represented by
the area of the smaller rectangle, which is found by multiplying length by
height. The length is the same as hours worked, and the height is the same as

the _____ _____ . Therefore, the area of the

rectangle and dollars of daily income will be   *(equal/unequal)*   . They will

both be equal to the number of _____ _____ times

the hourly _____ _____ .

2.22
If you worked four hours at a wage rate of $3 per hour, you would earn

$ _____. In Figure 2.3, this is represented by the _____
of the larger rectangle.

Answers
    20.   2 · 4 · 3
    21.   2 · wage rate · equal · hours worked · wage rate
    22.   12 · area

2.23   **Table 2.3**

WORK INCOME, TOTAL AND MARGINAL

Hours spent working	Total income	Marginal income
0	$ 0	
1	2	$2
2	4	2
3	6	2
4	8	2
5	10	2
6	12	2

In Figure 2.4, derived from Table 2.3, the points a, b, c, d, e, f, and g are all associated with the same wage rate of $ _____ per hour but with different numbers of _____ worked. The point b, for instance, is associated with one hour worked at $2 per hour. With what number of hours worked are a, d, and f associated? (a) _____ (d) _____ (f) _____ .

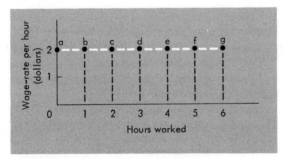

FIGURE 2.4   Wage rate and hours worked

2.24
As in Figure 2.3, the _____ of the various rectangles in Figure 2.4 will represent daily income from different numbers of _____ worked at a wage rate of $2 per hour.

Answers

23. 2 · hours · 0 · 3 · 5
24. areas · hours

2.25

The rectangle, for instance, whose corners are 0, 5, f, and a will have an area of

_____ units, representing an income of $ _____ . The

area is calculated by multiplying the length, _____ units, by the

height, _____ units. Daily income is calculated by multiplying

_____ _____ (on the horizontal axis) by a _____

_____ on the vertical axis.

2.26

What does the constant height of line ag indicate? It shows you for any
number of hours worked the income you would gain or lose by working one

hour more or one hour _____ . Thus, it shows you the

 (marginal/total)   income gained by working more or lost by working less.

Because the height is constant, the _____ income from working
is constant.

2.27

Let us now consider how to represent the marginal benefits from studying.
Table 2.4 repeats data from Chapter 1.

The third column gives your _____ income, that is, the income
gained from one extra hour of studying (or the income lost from one hour

_____ of studying).

2.28

If, instead of studying for one hour, you decide to study for two hours, your

total income from your father will increase from $ _____ to

$ _____ , that is, by $ _____ .

Answers

25. 10 · 10 · 5 · 2 ·   hours worked ·   wage rate
26. less · marginal · marginal
27. marginal · less
28. 4.32 · 8 · 3.68

Table 2.4

STUDY INCOME, TOTAL AND MARGINAL

Hours spent studying	Income from your father	Marginal income
0	$ 0	
		$4.32
1	4.32	
		3.68
2	8	
		3
3	11	
		2.32
4	13.32	
		1.68
5	15	
		1
6	16	

2.29

This increase in income is due to the additional hour of study or, in other words,

the _____ income in this example is $ _____ .

2.30

Proceeding in the opposite direction: If you were originally studying for two

hours per day, your daily income from your father would be $ _____ .
If you now decided to study one hour less, the daily income would fall to

$ _____ or decrease by $ _____.

2.31

Whether an increase from 1 to 2 in time spent studying or a decrease from 2 to

1, the marginal _____ gained or lost would be $ _____ .

Answers

29. marginal · 3.68
30. 8 · 4.32 · 3.68
31. income · 3.68

2.32

In Figure 2.5, where we have plotted data from Table 2.4, we show the relationship between hours spent studying and marginal income.

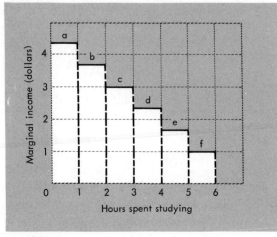

FIGURE 2.5   Marginal income from studying—I

In going from zero to one hour studying, total study income increases from

zero to $ _____ . This _____ income is represented

in Figure 2.5 by the rectangle a. The area of rectangle a is _____
units.

2.33

Adding another hour of studying (that is, bringing the total study time up to

two hours) adds $ _____ to study income. This marginal

_____ is represented by rectangle _____ , whose

area is _____ units.

2.34

Thus, total study income from two hours of studying will be the increase in

income from the first hour of studying plus the _____ in income

Answers

32.   4.32 · marginal · 4.32
33.   3.68 · income · b · 3.68
34.   increase

from the second hour of studying. In Figure 2.5, this will be the area of

rectangle a plus the area of rectangle b, or _____ units plus

_____ units, giving a total of _____ units.

2.35

Similarly, the sum of the areas of rectangles a, b, c, d, e, and f is the total

_____ from six hours of study. This total is $ _____ .

2.36

For simplicity, we have considered the marginal income associated with one-
hour changes in time spent studying. This has resulted in the step graph of
Figure 2.5. If we consider smaller time increments, for instance quarter
hours, we shall still have a step graph, but the steps will be ___(smaller/larger)___ ,

each hour now having _____ steps.

2.37

As we continue to take smaller and smaller time intervals on the horizontal
axis, the number of steps in the graph will ___(increase/decrease)___ , each succeeding
step becoming ___(smaller/larger)___ and ___(smaller/larger)___ .

2.38

As the steps become smaller, the graph comes closer to being a straight line.
If we divided the first hour, for instance, into minutes instead of quarter hours,

we would have _____ rectangles instead of 4, and if we divided it
into seconds, we would have 3,600. As we imagine subdividing the horizontal
axis into more and more, smaller and smaller units, for example milliseconds,

the graph will become closer and closer to being a _____ line as
in Figure 2.6.

Answers

34. 4.32 · 3.68 · 8
35. income · 16
36. smaller · four
37. increase · smaller · smaller
38. 60 · straight

2.39

In Figure 2.6, the line jk results from taking smaller and smaller intervals of the horizontal axis. The _____ under the line jk will represent study _____ from studying six hours.

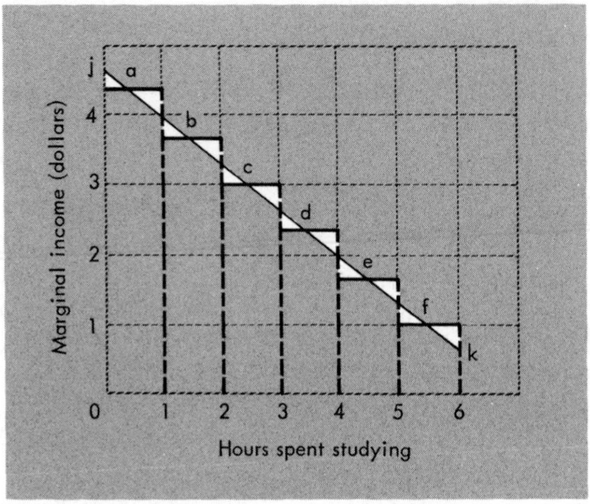

FIGURE 2.6   Marginal income from studying—II

2.40

This area will equal the _____ of the six rectangles a, b, c, d, e, and f. The unshaded areas now included by the line jk will equal the unshaded portions of each of the rectangles left outside by the line jk.

2.41

In Figure 2.7, the point s on line jk is associated with 2 hours of studying and a marginal income of _____ . The point t is associated with _____ hours of studying and a marginal income of _____ .

2.42

A movement from s to t occurs when you increase study time from _____ to _____ with a corresponding decrease in marginal income from _____ to _____ .

Answers

39. area · income
40. areas
41. 3 1/3 · 3 · 2 2/3
42. 2 · 3 · 3 1/3 · 2 2/3

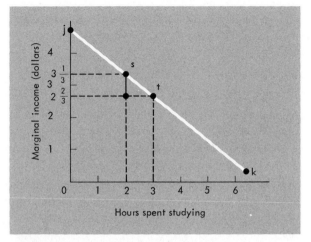

FIGURE 2.7   Marginal income from studying

2.43

As you increase hours studying, even though your marginal _____

decreases (that is, the line jk is negatively sloped), your total income _____ ,
that is, the area under the marginal income line, _(increases/decreases)_ from 0js2 to
0jt3.

2.44

Now reconsider Figure 2.4 (repeated here as Figure 2.8), which shows the
marginal gain from outside working or, because every hour of outside work
means one less hour studying, the marginal _(gain/cost)_ of studying.

Each additional hour spent studying means an hour _____ spent
working. Thus, the cost of an additional hour spent studying, that is, the

marginal cost of _(studying/working)_ , is the _____ forgone by not
working that hour. In this example, that cost is constant per hour and equal to

$ _____ . The area of the large rectangle 0ag6, which represents

the income forgone by not working at all, equals $ _____ . The

area of any of the smaller rectangles equals _____ forgone by not

working that extra hour, that is, the _____ _____ of
studying.

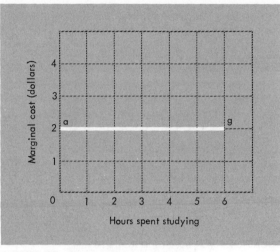

FIGURE 2.8   Marginal cost of studying

2.45

In order for any activity to be worth undertaking, its benefit must exceed the opportunity cost. As you will recall from Chapter 1, the benefit that could be

derived from the best alternative activity is the _____ cost. In deciding whether to study one hour, you must take into account the income forgone by not working that hour. The income forgone by not working is the

_____ cost of studying.

2.46

For example, if you were to study one hour, your study income would be

$4.32 but you would also lose $ _____ by not working that

hour. The benefit from studying one hour is $ _____ , while the

_____ cost is $2. Because the benefit from studying one hour is

__(greater/smaller)__ than the _____ _____ of

studying one hour, it __(will/will not)___ pay you to study at least one hour.

Answers

45. opportunity · opportunity
46. 2 · 4.32 · opportunity · greater · opportunity cost · will

2.47

With this in mind, consider Figure 2.9, which is a combination of the figures

with which you are familiar. The line jk shows the _____

income from studying, and line ag shows the _____ income
forgone by not working. The marginal income from studying is, of course,
the marginal ___*(benefit/cost)*___ of studying, and the marginal income for-

gone by not working is the marginal _____ of studying. At two
hours spent studying, the marginal benefit of studying is ___*(greater/less)*___
than the marginal cost.

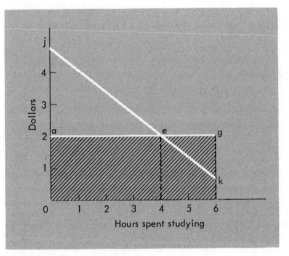

FIGURE 2.9   Study and work income

2.48
At point e, lines jk and ag intersect. This point e corresponds to _____
hours of studying.

2.49
To the left of e, that is, up to four hours of studying, the line jk lies *(above/below)*

the line ag, showing that the _____ income from studying is
___*(greater/less)*___ than the marginal income forgone by not working.

Answers
   47.   marginal · marginal · benefit · cost · greater
   48.   four
   49.   above · marginal · greater

2.50

Thus, at any point less than four hours of studying, your income will increase if

you spend more time _____ and less time _____ .

2.51

Above four hours of studying, however, the _____ benefit from
studying is _(greater/less)_ than the marginal cost of studying. At any
point above four hours of studying, it would pay you to _(increase/decrease)_
time spent studying. Only at four hours spent studying, where the

_____ benefit and cost are equal, will there be no incentive to
change the amount of time spent studying. Thus, the point where total

income from both studying and working is a maximum must be _____

hours studying and _____ hours working.

2.52

We have seen that the optimum, or best, position is where the _____

benefit and _____ cost are _____ . Only at such a
position will it be impossible to improve your position by making a change.

2.53

Whenever the marginal benefit of some activity exceeds the marginal cost, it will
pay to _(increase/decrease)_ that activity. And, whenever the marginal benefit falls
short of the marginal cost, the activity should be _(increased/decreased)_ .

2.54

This principle applies to any situation where a choice of different combinations
is involved. Taking more of one always involves giving up more of the other.

As a result, there will always be an opportunity _____ that must
be compared to the benefit of taking more of one. And the best combination

will be that for which the marginal _____ and marginal _____
are equal.

Answers

50. studying · working
51. marginal · less · decrease · marginal · four · two
52. marginal · marginal · equal
53. increase · decreased
54. cost · benefit · cost

REVIEW QUESTIONS

Questions 1 and 2 are based on the following diagram:

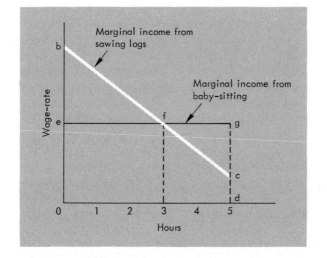

2.1
You have five hours to spend working. Which of the following statements are true?

a. The more time you spend sawing up logs, the less income you earn per hour of sawing.
b. The hourly wage rate you can earn babysitting is oe.
c. To maximize daily income, you would have to both saw logs and babysit.
d. All of the above.

2.2
You have five hours to spend working. Which of the following statements are true?

a. Daily income would be maximized by spending three hours sawing logs and two hours babysitting.
b. The maximum daily income you can earn is obfgd.
c. After three hours of log sawing, the marginal income from log sawing is less than the marginal income from babysitting.
d. All of the above.

Because the line bc is negatively inclined to the wage-rate axis, marginal income from log sawing decreases as time spent sawing increases. However, because the line eg is horizontal, marginal income from babysitting is constant and equal to oe per hour. The significance of those lines intersecting at f is that, after three hours of log sawing, additional time spent in the activity yields a lower marginal income compared with babysitting. Thus, to maximize income, you would spend three hours sawing logs (yielding an income of obf3) and two hours babysitting (yielding an income of 3fgd). The maximum daily income you can earn, therefore, is represented by the area obfgd. The correct response to both questions is d.

2.3

The government is considering an increase in expenditure for medical services. It should undertake this expenditure

a. if the total benefit derived from all medical services still exceeds the total cost.
b. if the total benefit derived from all medical services still exceeds that of any other good.
c. if the benefit from the extra medical services outweighs the cost of doing with less of other goods.
d. only if all of the above are true.

The real or opportunity cost of any good is what is given up to have that good. Efficiency in resource allocation is achieved when no resource, by being reallocated, could yield a greater benefit than it does in its current occupation. Thus, the government should increase medical services expenditure if and only if the benefit from the goods that must be given up does not outweigh the benefit from the additional medical services that have to be considered. (Note that only when the last dollar spent by the government on each possible service yields the same benefit will the total benefit from government expenditures not be increased by any reallocation.) The correct response is c.

2.4

A government has completed a cost-benefit study showing that the annual value of the services from an additional 100 miles of highway would be $4 million and the annual value of the services from an additional airport would be $3 million.

To achieve the most efficient use of resources, the government should

a. construct only 75 miles of highway (that is, 3/4 of 100).
b. construct only the 100 miles of highway.

c. construct both the 100 miles of highway and the airport.

d. not necessarily construct either any additional highway or the airport.

To maximize society's welfare, the government should allocate expenditure so that the marginal benefit from the last dollar spent on each good equals the marginal cost. If this condition did not hold, the government could increase welfare by reallocating its expenditure. Because no information is given about the costs of constructing highways or airports, it is impossible to tell whether carrying out either project, or both projects, would achieve an efficient use of resources. The correct response is d.

3

The Theory of Consumer Choice

3.1
In Chapters 1 and 2, we studied the principles of optimal resource allocation
that apply whenever you must choose among alternative uses for scarce
resources. In this chapter, we shall study how an individual allocates income
to make himself as well off as possible. For most individuals, income is a

scarce _____ to be allocated among many alternatives. In
economic jargon, we say that the individual attempts to maximize *utility*
(or satisfaction) subject to a *budget constraint*.

3.2
If, between the next two pages of this book, you found a dollar bill that was a
gift from me to you (this is purely hypothetical, you realize), how would you
spend it? The answer is fairly obvious; if you were a rational person, you would

spend it in such a way that you would receive maximum _____
(or satisfaction) from the dollar.

Answers
1. resource
2. utility

3.3
There exist many ways to spend the dollar. You have many wants you would
like to satisfy, and manufacturers have produced many commodities they
would like you to purchase. But you cannot buy them all; you cannot satisfy

all your _____ because you have a _____
constraint.

3.4
You will use your limited income, in this example $1, to purchase those
commodities that will satisfy you as completely as possible in such a situation.

That is, you will attempt to _____ your _____

subject to your _____ constraint.

3.5
You know better than anyone else what you like. Subject to legal considera-

tions, most people in this country are free to spend or allocate their _____
as they wish. As we shall see, it is the way that consumers like yourself allocate

their _____ that encourages manufacturers to produce the commodities people want most.

3.6
Manufacturers respond to consumers' preferences as expressed through their
spending habits. An economy operating in such fashion is said to allocate its

scarce _____ through a *free market*, or *free enterprise* system.

3.7
Some people argue that consumers do not always know their best interests,
and there should be limits on the way resources are allocated through a

_____ _____ system to reflect _____
wants. For instance, it is argued that horror comics should be banned because
they are not "good" for people. The same arguments are used in regard to
alcohol, cigarettes, and large automobiles. But in a free enterprise economy

Answers
3. wants · budget
4. maximize · utility · budget
5. income · incomes
6. resources
7. free enterprise · consumers'

like the United States, people __(do/do not)__ allocate part of their income to
the purchase of horror comics, alcohol, cigarettes, and large automobiles,
and, in response to consumers' spending, manufacturers __(do/do not)__
produce these goods.

3.8

Advocates of a completely free _____ system do not believe
consumers should be told what to buy or not to buy but believe that

individual _____ know their own interests best. We shall study
how consumers signal with dollar votes to indicate their *preferences* to

manufacturers. Manufacturers in turn hire scarce _____ and
produce the goods and services consumers want if profits are sufficient in
those fields of production. Manufacturers, we assume, are motivated by a
profit incentive, __(or/not)__ by their judgments as to what people should
buy. Consequently, in a free enterprise system, they will produce according

to consumers' _____ , only to the extent that this is consistent
with maximum profits for producers.

3.9

It is important to remember that manufacturers are concerned with people's
preferences only to the extent that those wants are backed by dollar votes.
You may prefer an expensive sports car to a standard four-door sedan, but
manufacturers will not be overly impressed by this preference unless you use

your _____ votes to express your preferences by actively
bidding in the market. In later chapters, we shall show under what circumstances
in a free enterprise system resources will be allocated in accordance with con-

sumer _____ as expressed by dollar votes.

3.10

Despite having many _____ , most consumers, for all practical
purposes, have limited means of satisfying them. Limited means for most
people take the form of limited incomes or limited budgets available for
expenditure on consumer goods and services. In any time period, we normally
assume, therefore, that each consumer (a consumer can be thought of as a
family unit as well as one individual) has a *budget constraint.* That is, we

Answers
  7. do · do
  8. enterprise · consumers · resources · not · preferences
  9. dollar · wants
  10. wants

assume the consumer is limited by his _____ from purchasing all
the goods and services he desires.

3.11
Within the limits of the budget constraint, however, the consumer attempts to
make his satisfaction or utility from consuming goods and services as large as
possible. Expressed more rigorously, we say that the rational consumer in any

time period attempts to maximize his utility subject to a _____

_____ .

3.12
Thus, a consumer will change his expenditure pattern if the change yields him

a higher level of _____ . He will continue to change his expendi-

ture patterns until he cannot _____ his total utility by a realloca-

tion of his expenditure. Only then will the consumer _____ his
total utility. And only then will the consumer be in equilibrium, that is, have
no incentive to alter his expenditure patterns.

3.13
When will the consumer be in equilibrium? As we shall see, he will be in
_____ when the utility he receives from the last dollar spent on
any good or service just equals the utility received from the last dollar spent

on any other good or service. Then and only then will he _____
his total utility.

3.14
After a certain point has been reached, the utility received from consuming
additional units of a good decreases for an individual. The extra utility
derived from consuming an additional unit of a good is known as the
marginal utility of that good. Thus, after a certain point has been reached in

the consumption of a good, the _____ _____ of that
good decreases as consumption increases.

Answers
  10. budget
  11. budget constraint
  12. utility · increase · maximize
  13. equilibrium · maximize
  14. marginal utility

3.15

Suppose, for instance, that after you have consumed a few beers in the local bar one evening, the utility you derive from, let us say, your fourth beer is less than that derived from your third. That is, as your consumption of beer

increases from three to four, your _____ utility decreases.

Suppose that the _____ derived from the fifth beer is even less than that from the fourth, and so on. It might be that a sixth beer may give you no utility or satisfaction at all and a seventh could give you pain rather than pleasure by making you sick. (You choose the numbers according to your capacity—it is the principle that is important!) This would be an example of negative utility from the seventh beer. You presumably would not consume a

seventh beer even if it were free, because you normally would want to _____ your total utility.

3.16

In this example, six beers would yield ___(more/less)___ utility than seven beers,

and when seven beers are consumed the _____ _____ becomes negative. This means that total utility decreases when a seventh beer is consumed; it does not mean that total utility is negative. _(true/false)_

3.17

In some given time period, how many beers will you consume if you have to pay for them? Given your income, we know that every beer you consume has

an opportunity cost, namely the _____ you give up by not using your income to buy other goods that you want. In deciding how much beer to buy, you will want to buy more beer as long as the marginal benefit is greater than the marginal cost of buying beer. That is, you will consume

additional beers until the last dollar spent on beer gives no more _____ . than the last dollar spent on any other good.

Answers

    15.   marginal · utility · maximize
    16.   more · marginal utility · true
    17.   utility · utility

3.18

To understand this point, consider the following example. If the last dollar

spent on a beer gives you less _____ than the last dollar spent on

a hamburger, then your total _____ will be higher if you consume
the hamburger rather than the beer. In general, you obviously __(will/will not)__
spend another dollar on good A if the utility received from that additional
consumption is less than the utility you would have received from the
additional consumption of an extra dollar's worth of some other good B.

3.19

It is only when the last dollar spent on each good yields the same utility that
(total/marginal) utility will be maximum.

3.20

In order to be in equilibrium consuming both hamburgers at 50 cents each and
beer at 25 cents a glass, the last hamburger consumed will have to yield you
(half the/the same/twice the) satisfaction of the last beer consumed. If 50 cents
spent on a hamburger gives you the same utility as 25 cents on a beer, you

should buy more _____ and fewer _____ . You will

maximize utility when the last dollar's worth of each yields the same _____ ,
or expressing this another way, when the marginal utility of beer divided by the

price of beer equals the _____ _____ of hamburgers
divided by the price of hamburgers. In this example,

$$\frac{MU\ beer}{25\cancel{c}} = \frac{MU\ hamburgers.}{50\cancel{c}}$$

For the ratio to be equal, the marginal utility of your last hamburger must be
__(twice/half)__ the marginal utility of your last beer.

Answers

18. utility · utility · will not
19. total
20. twice the · beer · hamburgers · utility · marginal utility · twice

3.21

How should you divide your income between any two goods A and B? As in the hamburger-beer example, if you want to maximize utility, you should consume two goods in such amounts that the last dollar spent on each good

yields the same _____ . Any different allocation of income will

yield a ___(smaller/larger)___ total utility.

3.22

Let us now suppose you were given additional income but were restricted still to spending all of it on goods A and B. With more income than before, you could now purchase more of each good, and, because you would be better off,

total _____ would be greater than before.

3.23

However, as you saw in the beer example, the _____ _____ of each good falls the more you buy. Consequently, when you regain a position

of equilibrium with your higher income buying _____ of each

good, the marginal utilities of each good will be _____ than before. In your new equilibrium position, however, it must still be true that

$$\frac{MU_A}{P_A} = \underline{\hspace{3cm}} .$$

3.24

Thus, given that you are restricted to only two commodities, and given that marginal utilities are positive, an increase in income will lead to an increase in

_____ utility; _____ utilities, however, will decline.

You will maximize _____ _____ when the last dollar's worth (or cent's worth) of expenditure on A yields the same satisfaction as the last dollar's worth of expenditure on B—in other words, when

$$\frac{MU_A}{\underline{\hspace{1cm}}} = \frac{\underline{\hspace{2cm}}}{P_B} .$$

3.25

Assume you are in equilibrium in this two-commodity world, so

$$\frac{MU_A}{P_A} = \frac{MU_B}{P_B} \; .$$

Now assume the price of commodity A falls; this will cause $\dfrac{MU_A}{P_A}$ to become

(less/greater) _____ than $\dfrac{MU_B}{P_B}$. To restore equality, that is, to make

$$\frac{MU_A}{P_A} = \frac{MU_B}{P_B}$$

you will reallocate your income between A and B, buying more _____

and less _____ than before.

3.26

As you consume more A, however, the marginal utility of each additional

unit consumed will _____ , and thus the ratio $\dfrac{MU_A}{P_A}$ will

_____ .As you consume less of B, conversely, the ratio $\dfrac{MU_B}{P_B}$

will _____ .

3.27

You will cease reallocating income when equality is restored; that is, when

$$\frac{MU_A}{P_A} = \text{_____} \; .$$

Then and only then will total _____ be a maximum.

Answers

25. greater · A · B
26. decrease · decrease · increase
27. $\dfrac{MU_B}{P_B}$ · utility

3.28

The last three frames have shown why the quantity that people would like to

buy if a good tends to be _____ at a lower price. This condition holds for most goods. Variables other than price, however, affect the quantity of any commodity purchased, and to fully understand, we must take into account all factors affecting consumers' purchases. Price, however, is one of

the most important variables, and we would expect people to buy _____ steak at $1 per pound than at $5 per pound.

3.29

Let us arbitrarily choose a time period of one week, and, given that you are a steak consumer, let us consider the factors that might influence the amount of steak you would purchase. The price of steak, one would expect, would certainly influence how much you purchase. And we would further expect

that the lower the price of steak, the _____ the amount of steak you would purchase.

3.30

One might also find, however, that if in a given week the local supermarket had lobster, chicken, and lamb at greatly reduced prices, you might buy no steak

during that week. Consequently, we would expect that the _____ of goods you might substitute for steak would affect the amount of steak you would buy.

3.31

Perhaps the only way you like your steak is barbecued outdoors over an oak chip fire. You also do not like to barbecue outdoors unless the weather is pleasant. Consequently, we would expect that if we chose a week in which the weather was predicted to be inclement, you would, in all probability, buy no steak that week. Thus, we can see that in this specific example the

amount of steak you might buy would depend upon the _____ . Pound for pound, sausage and hamburger tend to be cheaper than steak, and if indeed your income is very low, you might not be able to afford steak. Thus,

we would expect that _____ would be another factor that would influence the amount of steak you would buy.

Answers

28. greater · more
29. greater
30. prices
31. weather · income

3.32
We could expand the list of items that would affect the amount of steak you would buy in any given week, and we can see that the amount of steak demanded in any week depends not only on the price of steak buy also on many other factors. To the extent that those other factors are important in the determination of the amount of steak demanded, we cannot neglect all

factors except _____ when considering demand for steak.

3.33
Suppose we wished to explore the relationship between your demand for steak and the number of your guests. If you plan to serve each person half a pound of steak, then the relationship is simple.

Table 3.1

NUMBER OF GUESTS AND QUANTITY OF STEAK DEMANDED

Quantity of steak that would be bought (lbs)	Number of guests
½	0
1	1
1½	2
2	3
2½	4
3	5

Even if you have no guests, we are assuming you have a steak yourself. From

Table 3.1, we see that the quantity of steak that would be bought _____ as the number of guests increases.

3.34
Because we are concerned only with the relationship between your _____ for steak and the number of guests, we assume that anything else that could affect your demand for steak does not change during the time period under consideration. For instance, we assume the price of steak is fixed because if steak were to increase in price to $20 per pound after you bought one pound for $2 you would probably buy chicken rather than steak for your guests.

Answers
32. price
33. increases
34. demand

3.35

On the assumption that everything else remains unchanged, Figure 3.1

shows what quantity of _____ you would buy today for different

numbers of _____ .

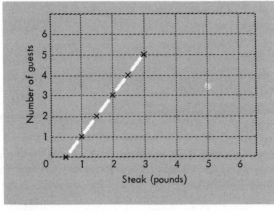

FIGURE 3.1   Demand for steak depending on number of
guests

3.36

We could repeat this process with all the items that affect your demand for
steak. If we were to draw graphs similar to Figure 3.1, we would have lines
that sloped upwards to the right, as in Figure 3.1, whenever the quantity of
steak demanded _(increased/decreased)_ along with the variable being considered.

In Figure 3.1, for instance, the quantity of steak demanded _____
as the number of guests increases.

3.37

If we choose an item for which the reverse relationship exists, for instance the
price of steak, we would have a graph that would be _(downward/upward)_
sloping to the _(left/right)_ because at higher prices smaller quantities of steak
would typically be demanded, other things remaining unchanged.

Answers

35. steak · guests
36. increased · increases
37. downward · right

3.38

Let us hold everything except the price and quantity of steak constant for now. By *everything* we mean all items we have considered and all items we have not considered that might affect the quantity of steak you would purchase in any given week. We wish to see the amount of steak you would purchase at different prices during a given week. If you look at Table 3.2, you will see

that if the price of steak were \$ _____ per pound or \$ _____ per pound, you would not purchase any steak during the week. You will also

see that if the price of steak were _____ , you would purchase more steak during that week.

Table 3.2

INDIVIDUAL DEMAND FOR STEAK

Prices per pound	Pounds of steak that would be purchased per week
\$5	0
4	0
3	1
2	2
1.50	3
1	5
.79	9
.50	15

3.39

In Figure 3.2, we have plotted the points from Table 3.2 and joined the points by a smooth curve. Points lying on the curve between any given points are approximations as to what you would buy if prices lay in between any of the quoted prices. We make this approximation in converting Table 3.2 into Figure 3.2 for the sake of simplicity.

Answers

38.   5 · 4 · lower

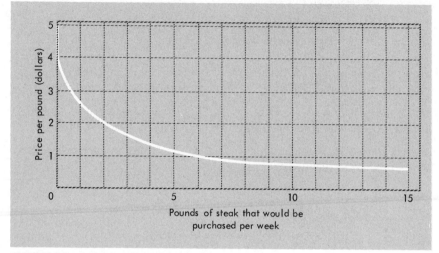

FIGURE 3.2   Individual demand for steak

What we have produced in Figure 3.2 is your individual _____
curve for steak for the specified week. And we can further see that at no two

different prices below $4 would the _____ of steak demanded by
you be the same.

3.40
Let us look carefully at Figure 3.2 because much more lies behind your

simple _____ _____ for steak than would appear.
First, there is a time period involved, which in this case happens to be one
week. However, if the time period became ten weeks instead of one week,
we would expect that the quantities of steak you would purchase at each of

the various prices in Table 3.2 would be _____ than the existing
quantities when the time period is one week. Consequently, the demand
curve in Figure 3.2 *(does/does not)*   reflect the situation in which the time
period is ten weeks.

3.41
Figure 3.2 says that holding everything else constant, you would in a given

week buy _____ pounds of steak if the price were $2 per

Answers
    39. demand · quantity
    40. demand curve · greater · does not
    41. two

pound, whereas you would buy _____ pounds of steak if the
price were $.79 per pound. If the price were $2.50 per pound, you would buy

between _____ and _____ pounds of steak.

3.42
Thus, if we hold everything else constant, we can tell from your _____

_____ how much steak you _____ buy at given prices.

3.43
Your demand curve for steak, therefore, is really a hypothetical curve showing

the quantities of steak you _____ buy at different prices

_____ everything else were held constant.

3.44
One day in your local supermarket, you are about to buy two pounds of
steak at $2 per pound when the attendant at the meat counter announces
that he is reducing the price of steak to $1 per pound. When this occurs, you
end up purchasing five pounds of steak. Has the meat attendant's decision to
change the price of steak from $2 per pound to $1 per pound changed your

demand curve? The answer is _____ . What you have done is
moved from one position on your demand curve to a new position on the same
demand curve. If everything else remains unchanged, then neither the position

nor the shape of your _____ in Figure 3.2 will change.

3.45
Let us now be more rigorous about the curve in Figure 3.2. First, we have a
given time period. Second, there are certain factors, such as your income,
number of guests, weather, and so on, that _(can/cannot)_ affect the
amount of steak you will buy in any week. Those factors, other than price,

Answers
41. nine · one · two
42. demand curve · would
43. would · if
44. no · demand curve
45. can

that influence the amount of steak you buy are parameters. In Figure 3.2, we assume that those _____ are fixed and do not change.

3.46

Thus, in Figure 3.2, we see that movements along this demand curve tell us

that the quantities that would be purchased _____ as price falls. Because prices and quantities change or vary, they are known as variables. Given that the parameters are fixed, we know that the quantity

is the dependent variable because the quantity taken will _____ on the price of steak.

3.47

It is highly unlikely, however, that the price of steak in the area in which you live will depend upon the quantity of steak you buy. And for this reason, __(price/quantity)__ is known as the independent variable. _(Price/Quantity)__ is known as the dependent variable.

3.48

The position and shape of the demand curve in Figure 3.2 will depend upon

the _____ , and if changes occur in any of the _____ , the position and shape of the demand curve will change. Because we will ultimately show how resource allocation in a price system responds to _____ preferences, it is important to know that some of the parameters determining the position of your demand curve in Figure 3.2 are your tastes and preferences.

3.49

Now, it is highly likely that parameters will change over time. For instance, it would be highly unusual if your tastes, income, and prices of all other goods were to remain unchanged over time. Consequently, it is highly unlikely that

Answers

45. parameters
46. increase · price · depend
47. price · Quantity
48. parameters · parameters · consumer

the position and the shape of your _____ _____ for steak will remain unchanged over time. But this change in the position and shape of your demand curve for steak over time must be carefully distinguished from a movement along your demand curve for steak in a given time period.

3.50

A demand curve is actually a hypothetical situation. It shows what would

happen, given the parameters, if the _____ of steak were to

change. That is, it tells us what _____ of steak you would buy

at various hypothetical prices, given no change in any of the _____ .

3.51

Let us consider a change in one of the _____ that will cause your demand curve to shift. A change in the price per pound of steak, all other things remaining unchanged, will cause your demand curve for steak to shift. *(true/false)*

3.52

If you look at your new demand schedule for steak alongside your original one (Figure 3.3), we can see there has been a(n) *(downward/upward)* shift of your demand curve, to the *(left/right)* . This has occurred because there has been a change in some of the parameters, for example a lowering of lamb and

chicken prices that determine the position of the _____ _____ , not because the price of steak has changed.

3.53

Let us now imagine that your income increases substantially. In considering your demand curve for steak, income is treated as a *(variable/parameter)* . With a higher income, you can now afford to buy more steak as well as more of many other goods. But if indeed you do buy more steak at the going price than you did with your original income, we would say there had been a *(shift of/movement along)* your demand curve.

Answers

49. demand curve
50. price · quantity · parameters
51. parameters · false
52. downward · left · demand curve
53. parameter · shift of

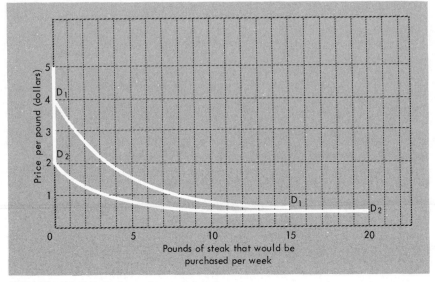

FIGURE 3.3   Shift in demand curve for steak

3.54

With your increase in income, you would now have a new _____

_____ for steak because one of the _____ , which
determine the position and shape of your demand curve, had changed. We would
expect this new demand curve to be to the _(right/left)_ of your old demand
curve.

3.55

In the blanks after each question, put the most appropriate statement concerning
your demand curve for steak. _(shifts to the right/shifts to the left/does not change)_

a. The price of lamb is drastically reduced, and you enjoy consuming lamb.

   _____

b. The price of lamb is drastically reduced, but you would buy lamb under no

   circumstances because you dislike it. _____

   _____

Answers

   54.   demand curve · parameters · right
   55.   a. shifts to the left
         b. does not change

c. Farmers are bringing fewer animals to the market, and consequently there is less steak in the stores. _____

_____

d. The government imposes a $.20 per pound tax on the price of steak. _____

_____

e. You are given a new barbecue as a gift and barbecuing weather is perfect.

_____

f. A friend of yours, who is a hunter, gives you a side of venison, and you have no freezer. _____

g. The supermarket has a special discount sale on steak. _____

_____

3.56
In Figures 3.2 and 3.3, we see that demand curves slope downward from

_____ to _____ . Or, in other words, the higher the

price of a good, other things remaining equal, the _____ the
quantity normally bought. Let us see why this should be so. The first and most
obvious reason is that at a lower price, given your income, you can afford to

buy _____ of that good because each unit costs less. If, for
instance, you have only $5, and the price of steak is $5 per pound, you could
buy only one pound of steak; whereas, if steak were $2.50 per pound, you

could buy _____ pounds of steak.

Answers
     c. does not change
     d. does not change
     e. shifts to the right
     f. shifts to the left
     g. does not change
  56. left · right · smaller · more · two

3.57

Second, at lower prices you tend to buy _____ of a good because this good now becomes relatively more appealing when compared to substitutes. Let us imagine that lamb and steak both sell for $1 per pound, and at those prices you buy one pound of each. Let us now imagine that the price of lamb does not change, but the price of steak falls to $0.50 per pound. You may well decide to buy more steak for the first reason, that is, steak is now cheaper and you can afford to buy more. But also, you may now decide to buy

_____ instead of lamb because the price of steak has _____ whereas the price of lamb has remained unchanged.

3.58

Another example would be the housewife who would prefer to cook with butter rather than oleomargarine, but who cannot afford to do so at existing prices. If

the price of butter falls, she can afford to buy _____ butter because of the price reduction. But she may also decide to cook now with butter, not because butter is even cheaper than oleomargarine at the reduced price, but because the relative difference in prices may be so small that she substitutes butter for oleomargarine in cooking.

3.59

There is still a third way we can look at our downward sloping demand curve, as we saw earlier in the chapter. In any given time period, the more of a good

consumed, the _____ the total utility, but the _____ the marginal utility.

3.60

The tendency to associate diminishing satisfaction or utility with each additional unit of a good consumed in a given time period is known as the *law of diminishing marginal utility*. The law of diminishing marginal utility essentially states that each additional unit of a good consumed within a given time period yields

diminishing _____ . This being the case, you *(will/will not)* be prepared to pay some fixed price per unit for additional units of this good. Consequently, we would expect that you will buy additional units only at a

_____ price.

Answers

57. more · steak · fallen
58. more
59. greater · smaller
60. utility · will not · lower

3.61

You will recall that earlier in this chapter you learned that you would be

maximizing total _____ if you allocated your budget in a two-commodity world so that

$$\frac{MU_A}{P_A} = \frac{MU_B}{P_B} .$$

3.62

Let us make clear the connection between utility theory and the demand curve. Imagine your daily budget is allocated between beer and hamburgers, the price of beer being 25 cents per glass and the price of each hamburger being 50

cents. In equilibrium, your utility will be _____ when

$$\frac{MU_B}{P_B} = \frac{MU_H}{P_H} .$$

3.63

Suppose that at the given prices

$$\frac{MU_B}{P_B} = \frac{MU_H}{P_H} = \frac{3}{1} .$$

That is,

$$\frac{MU_B}{PB} = \frac{3}{1}$$

and

$$\frac{MU_H}{P_H} = \text{_____} .$$

3.64

If the price of hamburgers is suddenly reduced to 25 cents each, then your $\dfrac{MU_H}{P_H}$

would become _____ .

Answers

61. utility
62. maximized
63. $\dfrac{3}{1}$
64. $\dfrac{3}{\frac{1}{2}}$

3.65
The correct answer is $\frac{3}{1\!\!\!/_2}$ or $\frac{6}{1}$; that is, the last 50 cents spent on hamburgers
will now yield approximately twice as much satisfaction as before because you
can now buy _____ hamburgers with 50 cents instead of one.

3.66
Thus, with the price reduction in hamburgers,

$$\frac{MU_H}{P_H} = \frac{6}{1}$$

and $\frac{MU_B}{P_B}$ will equal only _____ .

3.67
If you now spend 25 cents less on beer, your utility will fall by _____ . If
you spend 25 cents on another hamburger, your utility from the extra hamburger will be _____ . Thus, there will be a net gain in utility of 3 (+6-3) if
you reduce your expenditure on _____ and increase your
expenditure on _____ .

3.68
As you consume more hamburgers, however, $\frac{MU_H}{P_H}$ will _____
because of the *law of diminishing marginal* _____ . Simultaneously,
as you decrease your expenditure on beer, $\frac{MU_B}{P_B}$ will _____ .

3.69
You will continue to reallocate your expenditures until equilibrium is once more
attained. This will occur when

$$\frac{MU_H}{P_H} = \frac{MU_B}{P_B} .$$

Answers

65. 2

66. $\frac{3}{1}$

67. 3 · 6 · beer · hamburgers
68. decrease · utility · increase

Thus, you can see why your demand curve for hamburgers is negatively inclined;

that is why you will buy _____ hamburgers the lower the price. The same reasoning applies to beer or any other good.

3.70
So far, we have been concerned only with your demand curve for a product. It is unlikely that a manufacturer will be overly concerned with your demand

curve for his product because sales to you are probably so _____ as to appear negligible. One would *(expect/not expect)*   the owners of the local supermarket to be concerned with whether or not in any given day you purchase a loaf of bread, because the sale of one loaf of bread *(will/will not)*   substantially affect the sales or profits of the supermarket. This is an important assumption, but as you can well see a very reasonable one in a freely competitive economic system. In such a system, we assume that no individual can make any significant difference to the price of a good by purchasing or not purchasing in any given market. The influence of any individual in a market in a freely competitive economic system is *(negligible/substantial)* .

3.71
However, when we consider the total demand in any given market, we are summing up all the individual demands in this market, and we *(would expect/*

would not expect) manufacturers to be concerned with total demand. Total or market demand will be the subject of Chapter 4.

REVIEW QUESTIONS

3.1
When the prices of goods change, a consumer alters the quantities of goods he buys. As a result, an individual discovers that in the new situation marginal utilities are all lower than they were in the old situation. Which of the following is correct?

Answers
    69.   more
    70.   small · not expect · will not · negligible
    71.   would expect

a. The individual is better off, prices must have fallen on the average.
b. The individual is worse off, but prices could have fallen or risen on the average.
c. The individual is worse off, prices must have risen on the average.
d. Insufficient information is given to determine whether the individual is better off or worse off.

The principle of diminishing marginal utility states that, in a given time period, as an individual consumes more of a good, he derives less and less satisfaction from each extra unit consumed. Thus, in comparing the two situations, the lower marginal utilities, the greater the quantities that have been consumed. That is, lower marginal utilities mean greater total utility, that is, that the consumer is better off. The correct response is a.

3.2
A consumer buys only wine and cheese, and the more of any one he buys, the lower the marginal utility of that good. In spending all his income, his marginal utility of a bottle of wine is three and his marginal utility of a pound of cheese is one. The price of wine is $4 and the price of cheese is $2. If the consumer wants to maximize his utility, which of the following should he buy?

a. More wine and less cheese.
b. Less wine and more cheese.
c. More wine and more cheese.
d. Less wine and less cheese.

In allocating his income between any two commodities, for example cheese (C) and wine (W), the consumer will be maximizing his total utility when

$$\frac{MU_C}{P_C} = \frac{MU_W}{P_W}.$$

When this situation is reached, any reallocation of expenditure will make him worse off. However, in our example

$$\frac{MU_C}{P_C} = \frac{1}{2} \quad \left(\text{or } \frac{2}{4}\right) \quad \text{and} \quad \frac{MU_W}{P_W} = \frac{3}{4}$$

Because the ratios are unequal, he can become better off by reallocating his expenditures. If he spends $4 less on cheese, utility will decrease by two; if the $4 is now spent on wine, utility will increase by three, that is, net gain of one. As cheese purchases decrease, MU_C will rise, and as wine purchases increase, MU_W will fall. He should continue reallocating his income until the ratios are equal. The correct response is a.

3.3

A consumer's demand curve typically is downward sloping to the quantity axis for which of the following reasons?

1. At lower prices, the good in question is substituted for other goods that are now relatively more expensive.
2. At lower prices, the consumer can buy all he bought at the higher prices and with the money left over buy still more.

   a. 1 only
   b. 2 only
   c. Both 1 and 2
   d. Neither 1 nor 2

To the extent that goods are substitutes, consumers will substitute cheaper for more expensive goods in order to maximize utility. Starting from an equilibrium position where

$$\frac{MU_A}{P_A} = \frac{MU_B}{P_B} ,$$

if the price of A falls, then

$$\frac{MU_A}{P_A} > \frac{MU_B}{P_B} .$$

To restore equilibrium, less of B and more of A must be purchased.

   If the price of A falls, the consumer also experiences an increase in real income; he can now buy more of all goods, including the cheaper A. Marginal utilities will, of course, decrease as more of all goods are purchased, the consumer becoming better off. The correct response is c.

3.4

Which of the following is true with respect to a consumer's demand curve?

   a. The lower the price, the greater the marginal utility of the good.
   b. Prices of all other goods are assumed to be constant.
   c. It will shift to the right if the price of the good falls.
   d. It indicates what the going price of the good is.

The demand curve of a consumer for a commodity shows, for some given time period with everything else remaining constant, what quantities of the good the consumer would buy at different prices. It tells nothing about the going price of the good nor the marginal utility of the good. The correct response is b.

4

Market Demand

4.1

Aggregate demand schedules and curves are simply found by adding together

individual _____ schedules and curves.

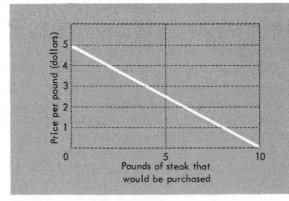

FIGURE 4.1   Family A's Demand for Steak

4.2

Table 4.1 and Figure 4.1 show family A's demand for steak in some given time period for a given set of parameters.

Table 4.1

FAMILY A'S DEMAND FOR STEAK

Price per pound	Pounds of steak that would be purchased
$5	0
4	2
3	4
2.50	5
2	6
1	8
0	10

As might be expected, the higher the price, the _____ the quantity that would be purchased.

4.3

Table 4.2 and Figure 4.2 show family B's demand for steak, again for some

given _____ period and given set of _____ , such as income and prices of other goods.

Table 4.2

FAMILY B'S DEMAND FOR STEAK

Price per pound	Pounds of steak that would be purchased
$5	0
2	5
1.50	7½
1	10
0	15

Answers

2. smaller
3. time · parameters

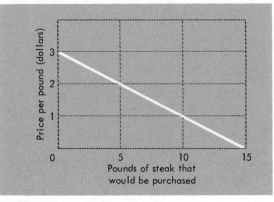

FIGURE 4.2 Family B's Demand for Steak

4.4

Family B's demand curve for steak _(is/is not)_ identical to family A's demand
curve. Although the slope of the curve is different, it remains true that the
(greater/smaller) the price, the greater the quantity demanded.

4.5

Let us now combine the two demand schedules. At $1 per pound, family A's
purchases would be eight pounds of steak, and at $1 per pound, family B's
purchases would be ten pounds. Therefore, taken together, both families

would purchase _____ pounds at $1 per pound. From Table 4.1
and 4.2, compute the quantities of steak that would be purchased by both
families at the following prices.

Prices	Quantities (Pounds)
$5	_____
3	_____
2	_____
1	_____18_____
0	_____

4.6

Figure 4.3 is derived in the same manner in which Figures 4.1 and 4.2 were derived; the relevant prices and quantities from your answers (the correct answers!) in frame 5 are plotted.

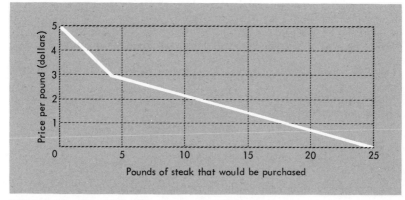

FIGURE 4.3   A's and B's demand curve for steak

The combined curve exhibits the same properties as the individual curves; the

higher the _____ , the smaller the quantity that would be purchased; or, for A and B to be willing to purchase larger quantities, there

must be _____ prices.

4.7

We could repeat the whole procedure for all steak buyers in some town

and arrive at the aggregate _____ schedule for steak for this community. This is the schedule that meat suppliers would be interested in.

4.8

In each demand curve we have considered so far, we have seen that at differ-

ent prices, _____ quantities are demanded. The concept that measures the responsiveness of the quantity demanded to price changes is

Answers

> 6. price · lower
> 7. demand
> 8. different

known as *price elasticity of demand*. *Price elasticity of demand* is defined in
the following way: price elasticity of demand = percentage change in quantity/
percentage change in price, which written symbolically is:

$$E_d \ (Price) = -\frac{\Delta Q}{Q} \bigg/ \frac{\Delta P}{P},$$

where Δ means "change in."

Because there is an inverse relationship between price and quantity

demanded, the ratio $\frac{\Delta Q}{Q} \bigg/ \frac{\Delta P}{P}$ would be _(positive/negative)_ . In order to make

elasticity a positive amount, elasticity is defined as follows:

$$E_d \ (price) = \underline{\hspace{2cm}} \bigg/ \underline{\hspace{2cm}}.$$

4.9

With price elasticity of demand, we are considering percentage change in

quantity and percentage change in _____ . If we wish to consider
income elasticity, we would measure the responsiveness of quantity taken to

income change. The identity would read: _____ elasticity of
demand = percentage change in quantity/percentage change in income or:

$$E_d \ (income) = \frac{\Delta Q}{Q} \bigg/ \frac{\Delta Y}{Y},$$

where Y represents _____ . Here the sign may be positive or
negative. The ratio is positive when increases in income are accompanied by
increases in the quantity purchased and when decreases in income are

accompanied by _____ in the quantity purchased. When an
inverse relationship exists, for example, income increases accompanied by

quantity purchased decreases, income elasticity of demand will be _____ .
Goods with such a property are called inferior goods. For many families,
cheap cuts of meat, low–quality wine, and tenement housing are examples

of _____ goods.

Answers

8.   negative · $-\dfrac{\Delta Q}{Q} \bigg/ \dfrac{\Delta P}{P}$

9.   price · income · income · decreases · negative · inferior

4.10
Unless we state otherwise, however, when we speak of elasticity of demand, we shall mean price elasticity of demand. Price elasticity of demand =

$-$ _____ / _____ .

4.11
The reason we are concerned with elasticity of demand is that we wish to

know, given a set of _____ determining the position of the demand curve for a good, how the quantity demanded will change as

_____ changes. Let us consider a good such as salt. Let us imagine that the typical housewife purchases one pound of salt every month and that one pound of salt costs 10 cents. Let us further imagine that the

price of salt rises to 20 cents per pound, that is, a _____ percent increase in the price of salt. What do you think will happen to the amount of salt purchased by the typical housewife in any month at the new price? Because salt is an essential purchase of the housewife for everyday cooking and is a trivial portion of her budget, in all probability the amount of salt purchased per month *(will/will not)* change a great deal.

4.12
Let us look at this in economic terms. If every housewife did not alter her purchase of salt at all, even though the price of salt doubles, we know that if we look at an aggregate demand curve for salt, we shall discover that the same

_____ would be purchased at the price of 10 cents per pound as at the price of 20 cents per pound. Or, saying the same thing, the amount of salt demanded at a price of 10 cents per pound *(is/is not)* the same as the amount demanded at 20 cents per pound.

4.13
Let us put the values from this example into the formula for price elasticity of demand ($-$ percentage change in quantity/percentage change in price). In this

example, the percentage change in quantity obviously equals _____ ,

Answers

10. percentage change in quantity/percentage change in price $(\frac{\Delta Q}{Q} / \frac{\Delta P}{P})$

11. parameters $\cdot$ price $\cdot$ 100 $\cdot$ will not

12. quantity $\cdot$ is

13. 0

and the percentage change in price equals _____ . Thus, the price
elasticity of demand for salt in going from a price of 10 cents per pound to a
price of 20 cents per pound equals −percentage change in quantity/percentage
change in price = _____ .

4.14
When we have a value for price elasticity of demand that is less than one, we say
we have *inelastic demand* over that range of prices. When we get a value equal to
one, we say we have *unitary elasticity of demand* over that price range, and
when we get a value greater than one, we say we have *elastic demand* over that
range of prices. Thus, in the example in the previous frame comparing price
of salt at 10 cents per pound and at 20 cents per pound and the corresponding
quantities purchased, we would say that demand over this range is *(inelastic/of*____
  unitary elasticity/elastic) .

4.15
What elasticity of demand really tells us is the responsiveness of quantities
that would be bought to changes in price. In our salt example, the responsiveness of the quantity of salt that would be bought given the change of price we

considered was _____ , and consequently in this price range demand

was _____ .

4.16
As you might guess, at the other end of the spectrum, if a relatively small
change in price brings about a relatively large change in the quantity that

would be demanded, we would say that demand was _____ in
that range of prices.

4.17
Our third case would occur when a 1 percent increase in price would bring
about a 1 percent *(increase/decrease)* in the quantity that would be demanded.

We would say that in this case elasticity of demand is _____ .

Answers
  13.   100 · 0
  14.   inelastic
  15.   zero · inelastic
  16.   elastic
  17.   decrease · unitary (one)

4.18

Let us choose a couple of examples to see whether the demand is elastic or inelastic over given price ranges. Imagine that the makers of a popular brand of cigarettes, such as Kansers, were to increase the price of Kansers cigarettes by 10 cents per pack, and further assume that the price of all other cigarettes did not alter. Now, because many people believe that any one brand of cigarettes has several close substitutes, we would expect smokers to switch from Kansers to some other brand of cigarettes. If this were to occur, then

sales of Kansers cigarettes would _____ because of the price

increase, which would cause people to switch to close _____ .

4.19

If the observed percentage decrease in the quantity of Kansers cigarettes demanded were greater than the percentage increase in price, we would say

that the demand for Kansers cigarettes was _____ over this price range.

4.20

Let us imagine the reverse situation. Imagine Kansers are reduced by a few cents per pack, and this causes many people who normally smoke other brands to switch to Kansers. In this case, the percentage *(increase/decrease)* in quantity bought would be large, whereas the percentage *(increase/decrease)* in price would be small. Over this price range, we would again say that the

demand for Kansers cigarettes was _____ .

4.21

If a 1 percent decrease in the price of Kansers cigarettes led to only 1 percent

_____ in the quantity of Kansers bought, the demand for Kansers cigarettes over this price range would be of unitary elasticity.

Answers

18. decrease · substitutes
19. elastic
20. increase · decrease · elastic
21. increase

4.22
Consider the following, however. If a small increase in the price of all cigarettes had a negligible effect on the quantity of cigarettes demanded, *ceteris paribus* (with other things remaining equal), the demand for cigarettes

would be _____ over this price range, even though the demand for any particular brand were elastic over the same price range.

4.23
Although economists cannot tell why some people prefer good A over good B and why other people prefer good B over good A, general statements can be made about when demand for a product is likely to be elastic over some price range and when demand is likely to be inelastic over a price range. When we discussed salt, we argued that the demand for salt over moderate price changes

was likely to be _____ , one reason being that salt normally consumes a negligible portion of a family's income. This means that a small change in price *(would/would not)*   significantly alter the amount of salt the typical housewife purchased.

4.24
For most people, salt is also a necessity, and there are very few items one can substitute for salt in the kitchen. We can take our salt example and generalize

it by saying the demand for a good is likely to be _____ when expenditure on that good consumes a very small portion of the weekly income

or weekly budget and demand is also likely to be _____ when the good in question has no close substitute.

4.25
An example of a necessity would be your urgent need of the services of a dentist or surgeon. If you required an appendectomy, and if a hospital attendant were to tell you that the surgeon's fee for performing the appendectomy was $200, you would in all probability agree to have the operation performed. If, however, the hospital attendant then told you that he had made an error

Answers
22.   inelastic
23.   inelastic   ·   would not
24.   inelastic   ·   inelastic

and the surgeon's fee was $225, it is highly unlikely that you would change
your mind about the operation. In this example, therefore, the demand for a

surgeon's services is _____ , implying that for a given moderate
price change, the amount of a surgeon's services demanded *(will/will not)*
vary significantly with the prices charged.

4.26
Goods that are consumed together are known as complementary goods. Left

shoes and right shoes are examples of _____ goods, whereas yellow

pencils and blue pencils are _____ goods. As we might expect, the
demand for many complementary goods is inelastic. One requires gasoline
before one can drive an automobile; because one is consuming gasoline as one

consumes an automobile's services, automobiles and gasoline are _____
goods.

4.27
If the price of gasoline were to increase a few cents per gallon, one
(would/would not) expect sales of gasoline to fall significantly. If this were to

be the case, the demand for gasoline would be _____ . However,

one brand of gasoline is a very close _____ for another brand of
gasoline. And if indeed the price of one brand of gasoline were to increase but
all others were to remain unaltered, we would expect sales of the higher-priced

brand to _____ significantly. Thus, a good that has very close

substitutes tends to be characterized by an _____ demand.

4.28
From the previous frames, we can draw important inferences. If we are dealing
with one good for which there is no close substitute, demand is likely to be

_____ , but if we are dealing with a brand of good for which there

are very close substitutes, demand for that brand is likely to be _____ .

Answers
   25. inelastic · will not
   26. complementary · substitute · complementary
   27. would not · inelastic · substitute · decrease · elastic
   28. inelastic · elastic

4.29

Demand is likely to be _____ where

a. the amount of money involved is very small.
b. no close substitutes are available.
c. the buying of this good cannot be postponed.
d. there is a large variety of possible uses for this good.

It should be remembered in discussing elasticity of demand that we are

considering relatively _____ price changes.

4.30

How would you classify the following goods—as complements or substitutes?

a. Automobile tires and automobiles minus tires   _____

b. Black and white films and color films   _____

c. A film and a camera   _____

d. Two $5 bills and a $10 bill   _____

e. Coca Cola and Pepsi Cola   _____

f. Shirts and trousers   _____

4.31

Let us now explore the importance of elasticity and inelasticity. Let us consider
the case of one good: light bulbs have very few close substitutes, we would

expect the demand for them to be _____ . Let us now imagine
that all manufacturers of light bulbs got together (colluded) and decided to
increase the price of all light bulbs by 10 percent.

4.32

Because the demand for light bulbs is relatively _____ , we would
not expect there to be a significant _____ in the quantity of light
bulbs purchased; and consequently we would expect that the total income

Answers

    29. inelastic · small
    30. complements · substitutes · complements · substitutes · substitutes
         complements
    31. inelastic
    32. inelastic · reduction

manufacturers of light bulbs would receive after they started charging the

higher price would be _____ than it was before. This would occur because the price had risen, whereas the quantity purchased had changed *(more than/less than)* proportionately. Consequently, the total revenue (price X

quantity) received from the sale of light bulbs would _____ .

4.33
Total revenue is a technical term used by economists to describe, in this example, the total income received from the sale of light bulbs, and, as you might expect, we calculate total revenue by multiplying the number of

light bulbs sold by the _____ of light bulbs.

4.34
Thus, we see that in situations where demand is inelastic, total revenue will move in the same direction as price. If price is increased, total revenue will

_____ , whereas if price is decreased, total revenue will _____ .

4.35
Let us choose another example that shows the importance of the concept of price elasticity in a policy setting. As you probably know, the price airlines can charge for tickets between any two cities is set by the Civil Aeronautics Board (C.A.B.). Recently, in response to low passenger loads and falling profits the airlines sought a fare increase. Now, if the demand for airline travel by prospective passengers were *inelastic,* the percentage increase in

fares would be _____ than the percentage decrease in passengers.

4.36
This was obviously the assumption the airlines were making. Why? The total money or revenue an airline receives for a flight equals the number of passengers times the price of an airline ticket. There are several ways for a flight's revenue to increase: more passengers with a constant price; more passengers with a higher price; and fewer passengers with a higher price if,

and only if, the proportional decrease in the number of passengers is _____

Answers
32. greater · less than · increase
33. price
34. increase · decrease
35. greater
36. less

than the proportional increase in price. But, of course, this is the definition of

_____ demand, which the airlines had to be assuming in seeking
a price increase.

4.37
As an example, suppose the existing round trip fare between two cities is $100
and at this price an airline flies 200 passengers per day on this route. Total
revenue, which is found by multiplying the price, or fare, by the _____

of _____ equals $ _____ .

4.38
If, in response to the airline's request for a fare increase, the C.A.B. allows
a 10 percent rise to $110 and the airline discovers that although fewer
passengers now fly, total fare revenue rises, for example, 190 passengers
at $110 equals $20,900, then, other things remaining unchanged, we would
conclude that the demand for airline travel within the range of prices on the

route was _____ . Thus, though _____ passengers
now fly, total fare revenue has risen because the proportional increase in

fare is _____ than the proportional _____ in the
number of passengers.

4.39
On the other hand, if the increase in fare to $110 led to only 150 passengers
per day, total fare revenue would decrease to $16,500. Demand would there-

fore be _____ because the proportional increase in fare is

_____ than the proportional decrease in passengers.

4.40
The third possibility would occur when the fare increase was matched proportionately by a passenger decrease. In this case, the demand would be of

_____ _____ , and total _____ _____
would remain unchanged.

Answers
36. inelastic
37. number · passengers · 20,000
38. inelastic · fewer · greater · decrease
39. elastic · less
40. unitary elasticity · fare revenue

4.41
Thus, if the airline wishes to maximize total fare revenue, it should seek a fare _____ if it believes the demand to be inelastic. By similar reasoning, it should seek a fare _____ if it believes the demand to be elastic.

4.42
It may well be that regularly scheduled airlines today find themselves in a quandary. Many private clubs and organizations charter airplanes to fly members to, say, Europe. They tend to charge each member the cost of chartering the plane divided by the number of passengers. If the plane is full, the round-trip price to London from the West Coast for a passenger is around $200 to $250. This is much less then the $838 fare set by international agreement for regularly scheduled flights (passengers, of course, on regularly scheduled flights have a wide choice of flight times, airlines, and routes compared with charter flights). Now, if demand for such travel is price elastic, and if regular airlines wish to increase total fare revenue, they should seek a fare _____ . The problem arises because it is highly probable that for other passengers—many businessmen, for example—the demand is inelastic and consequently a fare decrease would reduce total _____ _____ for this group.

4.43
Diagrammatically, the problem can be seen in Figure 4.4,

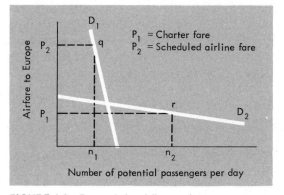

FIGURE 4.4 Demands for airline services

Answers
41. increase · decrease
42. decrease · fare revenue

where D_1 is the demand of businessmen for regularly scheduled international airlines and D_2 the demand of vacationers. Total daily fare revenue for international airlines equals area op_2qn_1, that is, fare times the number of passengers. If, at prices around p_2, demand is price inelastic, the area representing total fare revenue would _____ if fares were raised.

4.44

Area op_1rn_2 represents charter fare revenue and is found by multiplying the fare of _____ by the number of passengers _____ .
If, at prices around p_1 demand is price elastic, area op_1rn_2 would increase if fares were _____ .

4.45

What should the airline policy be? Many airlines are flying planes less than one-half full on several routes. They would like to fill those empty seats with fare-paying passengers to _____ total fare revenue. They do not want a decreased fare for passengers whose demand is price _____ ;
they would undoubtedly want a decrease in fare for passengers whose demand is _____ because, if both groups could be isolated and not allowed to trade tickets, total fare revenue would _____ .

4.46

Do students and servicemen have price elastic demands for airline travel? The answer would appear to be _(yes/no)_ if you consider the airline's policy of encouraging the C.A.B. to have special reduced fares for both groups. Similarly, the airline seeking lower fares for special summer flights to Europe is an indication that they believe the demands of many summer travelers are price _____ .

4.47

For most businessmen going to Europe, there is no close substitute to flying.

Traveling by sea takes up too much time—the opportunity _____ is too high. Consequently, we would expect the demand for airline travel for this group to be price _____ .

Answers

43. increase
44. op_1 · on_2 · lowered
45. increase · inelastic · elastic · increase
46. yes · elastic
47. cost · inelastic

4.48

For the summer traveler, however, there are many ways to spend a vacation without going to Europe. Camping in the mountains, traveling across country

by car, and trips to the beach are _____ to vacationing in Europe, and, as we discussed previously, the demand for substitutes is likely to be price

_____ .

4.49

To the extent that people taking a vacation can arrange a convenient charter

flight, the method of traveling becomes a close _____ for commercial flights. Because there exists a large price differential between the charter and commercial flight, the opportunity to buy charter flight tickets encourages _____ people to fly and also causes a switch from commercial flights to charter flights.

4.50

The demand curves we have considered so far we would describe as normal

demand curves. Those curves slope downwards from _____ to

_____ , indicating that at higher prices a _____ quantity would be purchased.

4.51

Just as there are exceptions to most rules, so there are exceptions to our normal demand curves. Some people believe (often for good reasons) that "you only get what you pay for," and if they see a good priced lower than what they expect it to be, they may have some doubts as to the quality of this good, whereas if this good were priced higher, they might be prepared to buy it. Thus, this could lead to a situation that would be the reverse of our normal demand curve situation. At a higher price, people would actually

buy _____ of the good than they would at a lower price, and consequently, the demand curve for this good for the group of people who think in this fashion *(would/would not)* slope downwards from left to right.

Answers

48. substitutes · elastic
49. substitute · more
50. left · right · smaller
51. more · would not

4.52

Similar to this type of situation is the situation involving prestige goods. Prestige goods, such as mink coats, may be bought by some people simply

because the price of mink coats tends to be relatively _____ . If the price of mink coats were very low and many people had them, mink coats

would no longer be a _____ good, and consequently, those people who buy them for prestige reasons would not purchase them at lower prices. Again, we would have an example of a demand curve for mink coats by this

group of people that would not slope _____ from left to right. In such examples, you might want to argue that other things are not being held constant and thus we are really not discussing only one demand curve in each case. This would be a legitimate objection; it would remain true, however,

that plotting of points on a graph could yield a _____ inclined curve.

4.53

There is another famous case of a nonnormal sloping demand curve, involving an inferior good, which refers to the demand for potatoes by Irish peasants. You should recall that an inferior good is a good whose income elasticity of demand is *(negative/positive)* , that is, where increases in income (+) are associated with decreases in quantities purchased (−). Irish peasants were very poor people who could only afford to buy very cheap food, and potatoes comprised a substantial portion of their normal diet. In good times, however, when Irish farmers had bumper crops of potatoes, the price of potatoes tended to fall. Because potatoes consumed a large portion of the Irish income or budget for the typical peasant family, a fall in the price of potatoes would mean that each family could buy the same quantity of potatoes as they

normally did at the higher price for _____ money. Consequently, they would have *(some/no)* income left to spend on other goods after their purchase of potatoes.

4.54

With this income, the Irish peasant could now afford to buy other goods such as meat, milk, and cheese. But because families could now enjoy meat, milk, and cheese, they did not require as many potatoes, and consequently the peasants would buy fewer potatoes. Here we have an example that shows that

through a _____ in the price of potatoes, Irish peasants could

Answers

52. high · prestige · downwards · positively
53. negative · less · some
54. fall

afford to buy some expensive foods, and consequently, would eat _____
potatoes. In terms of the demand curve for potatoes, we can see that at a

lower price, _____ potatoes were purchased than previously, at
the higher price. Again, we have an exception to the rule where the demand
curve, for potatoes in this instance, __(does/does not)__ slope downwards from
left to right. From demand let us now turn our attention to supply.

REVIEW QUESTIONS

4.1
This question is based on the following hypothetical statement:
    "An electrical power utility requests that the Federal Power Commission
(FPC) approve an increase in rates for electricity in order to increase its
revenues to overcome falling profits. The FPC disapproves the increase and
suggests that the utility would do better if it reduced its rates."
    On the basis of the above statement, which of the following is true?

a. The utility will not be able to increase its revenues, because it cannot
   raise its rates.
b. The utility believes the demand for power is inelastic; the FPC believes
   demand is elastic.
c. The utility believes the demand for power is elastic; the FPC believes
   demand is inelastic.
d. On the basis of this statement none of the above can be true.

When demand is inelastic, an increase in price leads to an increase in revenue.
When demand is elastic, a decrease in price leads to an increase in revenue.
Because the utility wants a price increase, it presumably believes demand is
inelastic. And as the FPC suggests a price decrease, it presumably believes
demand is elastic. The correct response is b.

4.2
Which of the following statements would be correct if the demand for the
good in question were inelastic?

1. Government sponsored agricultural research that increased acreage
   yields would lead to a decline in farmers' incomes.
2. Burning part of the coffee crop by the Brazilian government in years
   of large supply would keep export earnings from falling.

Answers
    54. fewer · fewer · does not

a. 1 only
b. 2 only
c. both 1 and 2
d. neither 1 nor 2

When demand is inelastic, it means that as you move along the demand curve, the percentage change in price is greater in absolute value than the percentage change in quantity. When demand is inelastic, an increase in quantity will result in a decline in total revenue (price times quantity) because the rise in quantity will be more than offset by the decline in price. If government agricultural research increases farm productivity, farm output would rise and farm prices would fall. With an inelastic demand, total revenue would fall. If revenue fell more than costs, farmers would suffer a loss in income. Similarly, if demand is inelastic, the burning of coffee when output of coffee increases would prevent revenue from falling. The correct response is c.

4.3
In traveling about a city, most people use either subway or bus. Suppose all subway fares were doubled, but bus fares remained unchanged. How would the subway fare increase affect the total fare revenue?

a. It would increase for buses but might increase or decrease for subways.
b. It would increase for subways but might increase or decrease for buses.
c. It would increase for both subways and buses.
d. It would increase for subways and remain unchanged for buses.

As subway fares increase, some people will switch to substitute goods, in this case, buses. Thus, total bus revenue will increase. Total subway fare revenue will increase if the percentage fare increase exceeds the percentage subway passenger loss, that is, if the demand for subway services in the relevant price range is inelastic. If the demand is price elastic (or of unitary elasticity), subway fare revenue will not increase as subway fares increase. The stem of the question attempts to point out that buses and subways are substitutes. Were they complements, for example, if passengers used buses to reach subway stations, then, assuming the demand for subway services is not perfectly inelastic, bus revenue would fall as subway fares increased, because traveling on both would be reduced. Again, subway revenue would rise or fall depending on the price elasticity of demand. The correct response is a.

4.4
Several baseball teams are considering allowing persons 65 years of age or older to attend games for $1 instead of the usual $3.

If the gate receipts were to rise with the adoption of the proposed policy, which of the following statements must be true?

1. As a group, older people would have as a result more income to spend on all other commodities.
2. The quantity of tickets bought by older persons is more responsive to changes in price than the quantity bought by younger persons.
3. The resulting increase in revenue from new fans would exceed the resulting loss in revenue from existing fans who would pay $1 instead of $3.

   a. 1 and 2 only
   b. 2 and 3 only
   c. 3 only
   d. 1, 2, and 3

One would expect that, other things being equal, a lower price for tickets for older persons would mean a larger quantity bought by older persons. If, at the lower price, gate receipts are higher, it means that the proportionate decrease in price is less than the proportionate increase in tickets sold; that is, the revenue gained from the new fans exceeds the revenue lost from old fans who now pay less for their tickets. Technically, in the relevant price range, older persons' demand for tickets is price elastic. Because the question refers to price reductions only for older people, the increase in revenue to the team will come only from older people. Because as a group they now spend more on baseball, they will have less to spend on all other commodities but will, of course, experience an increase in real income. Nothing is known about the price elasticity of demand for tickets of younger persons, and, consequently, no comparison can be made. The correct response is c.

5

Productivity and Costs

5.1
In many ways, a supply curve is similar to a demand curve. Each describes a relationship between the quantity and the price of a commodity. However, whereas a demand curve tells the quantities of a good that would be

_____ in any time period in any given market at different prices, a supply curve tells the quantities of a good that would be supplied

in any given time period in any given market at various _____ .

5.2
A supply curve is similar to a demand curve in that it represents a set of hypothetical situations. It shows how much of a good suppliers would offer

for a sale in a given market in a given _____ _____

in response to various _____ .

Answers
1. demanded · prices
2. time period · prices

5.3

As in the case of the demand curve, the position of the supply curve is fixed

by a set of _____ , which are factors that influence supply but

which are assumed to be _(variable/constant)_ . The two variables are again price

and quantity, price being the independent variable and quantity that would be

supplied being the _____ variable.

5.4

We saw in discussing demand curves that normally the higher the price, the

_____ the quantity that will be demanded, and, consequently,

most demand curves slope _____ from left to right.

5.5

In the case of a supply curve, the reverse is true. Normally, in a given time

period, suppliers will be willing to supply more of a good only at a _____

price, *ceteris paribus.* Typically, therefore, supply curves slope _____

from left to right.

5.6

The suppliers of goods and services (output) in our economy face three basic
problems:

a. How much output should they produce per time period?
b. What price should they charge for each unit of output?
c. What is the most efficient way to produce that output?

To fully understand the behavior of suppliers (and why supply curves

typically slope _____ from left to right), we must study productivity and costs. More simply expressed, we must study how much output
will result from different amounts and combinations of inputs—this is the
study of productivity—and also how much it will cost to produce such outputs.

Answers

3. parameters · constant · dependent
4. smaller · downward
5. higher · upward
6. upward

5.7
Consider Table 5.1, which shows data on what would happen if, *ceteris paribus,*
a farmer were to vary the amounts of labor input, which we are measuring in

Table 5.1

WHEAT OUTPUT—ONE FIELD WITH VARYING LABOR INPUT

Units of labor input (man-days)	Total product (bushels)	Average product per unit of labor input (bushels)	Marginal product of labor input (bushels)
0	0	—	40
1	40	40	100
2	140	70	160
3	300	100	180
4	480	120	170
5	650	130	160
6	810	135	150
7	960	137	120
8	1,080	135	90
9	1,170	130	30
10	1,200	120	−10
11	1,190	108	−50
12	1,140	95	−230
13	910	70	

_____ , in one of his wheat fields. Labor is not the only factor of
production involved in the production of wheat, but here we are holding all other

inputs, or factors of _____ , constant, and we are asking what
happens when we vary only one input, in this case labor. That is, we are hold-

ing _____ such things as the amount of fertilizer and the amount
of mechanical aids a farmer might use.

5.8
Consider only the first two columns. We can see that as we add successive

inputs of labor, total output (product) rises until we add the _____

unit of labor. Beyond that point, total output _____ and continues
to do so, the more labor input we use.

Answers
    7. man-days · production · constant
    8. eleventh · decreases

5.9

If the farmer were to employ more than 10 units of labor input, total output would be *(more/less)* _____ than total output with 10 units of labor input. We could imagine workers getting in each other's way. Consequently, it ___*(would/*

_*would not)*___ be profitable for the farmer to hire this eleventh unit of labor input as long as he has to pay a positive price for each unit of labor input.

5.10

In our example, therefore, maximum total output can be obtained when the

farmer uses _____ units of labor input. This maximum is

_____ bushels of wheat.

5.11

Column 3 is derived by dividing the figures in column _____ by

the corresponding figures in column _____ . Column 3, which is

also in bushels, is a measure of the _____ _____ per
unit of labor input.

5.12

In column 3, we can see that the average product per unit of labor input

increases up to the _____ unit of labor input, whereafter it

_____ .

5.13

Column 4 measures the marginal product of labor input, also in bushels.
This column tells us what the incremental, or additional, or marginal output
will be if we add one more unit of labor input. For instance, if we consider

the first two lines, total output from zero units of labor input is _____

bushels. Total output from one unit of labor input is _____
bushels. Thus, we can see that the increase in output in going from zero units
of labor input to one unit of labor input (that is, the additional or marginal

product) is _____ bushels.

Answers

9. less · would not
10. 10 · 1,200
11. 2 · 1 · average product
12. seventh · decreases
13. 0 · 40 · 40

5.14

We see also that the total output from employing three units of labor input is

_____ bushels, and total output from employing four units of

labor input is _____ bushels. Thus, the difference between those

totals, in this case _____ bushels of wheat, is due to the addi-

tion of the _____ unit of labor input. Consequently, we would

say that the _____ _____ of the fourth unit of

labor input is _____ bushels.

5.15

Now consider the output from nine units of labor input; it is _____
bushels. Adding one more unit, the tenth unit, gives us only a very small

increase in total output—an increase in total output of _____

units of wheat. Thus, we see that the _____ _____

of the tenth unit of labor input is, in this case, _____ bushels.

5.16

When we add an eleventh unit of labor input, we see that total output

actually _____ from _____ bushels to _____
bushels.

5.17

Thus, the output attributable to the eleventh unit of labor input, that is,

the _____ _____ of the eleventh unit, is negative in

the amount of _____ bushels.

5.18

After the eleventh unit of labor input, as more labor is added, total product

continues to _____ . The marginal product of each successive unit

added remains _____ and becomes smaller and smaller.

Answers

14.   300 · 480 · 180 · fourth · marginal product · 180
15.   1,170 · 30 · marginal product · 30
16.   decreases · 1,200 · 1,190
17.   marginal product · 10
18.   decrease · negative

5.19

The data in Table 5.1 on the marginal product of labor provide an example of the widely observed phenomenon of *diminishing returns*. After some point has been reached, the amount of *additional* output obtained through adding more units of one factor input to a fixed supply of other factors will decrease. We saw this to be true in Table 5.1. We held constant all factors of production except _____ , and we observed as we added successive units of labor that, after a point was reached, the additional output, or _____ _____ , of each successive unit of labor input _____ .

5.20

Thus, we would say that this is an example of _____ _____ because as the proportion of one factor input to other fixed factor inputs is increased, the _____ product of this factor input will, after a certain point has been reached, decrease and continue to decrease.

5.21

The decrease in the marginal product will ultimately result in a decrease in the _____ product of the factor input that is being added. While the marginal product is above the average product, the average product will _(increase/decrease)_ . When the marginal product is below the average product, the average product will _(increase/decrease)_ . The marginal product will equal the average product when the average product is at a maximum.

5.22

It should be obvious that under normal circumstances we would never expect an entrepreneur, paying positive prices for his factor inputs, to hire an additional unit of some specific input whose marginal product was zero or _____ . Is the following statement true or false? We would, therefore, never expect an entrepreneur to hire an additional unit of any input if the marginal product of this unit were less than the marginal product of all other hired units. _____

Answers

19. labor · marginal product · decreased
20. diminishing returns · marginal
21. average · increase · decrease
22. negative · false

5.23

Do we know how many units of labor input the farmer should hire if he wishes to maximize his wheat output? _(yes/no)_ . Do we know how many units of labor input the farmer should hire to make as high a profit as possible? _(yes/no)_ .

5.24

Consider the following piece of information, however. Imagine that you are told that the farmer has to pay each man 30 bushels of wheat for a day's work. That is, the extra cost to the farmer of each additional man-day hired

equals _____ bushels. What is the marginal benefit to the farmer of each additional man-day hired? The marginal benefit is the additional out-

put produced or the _____ _____ of labor input.

5.25

As you will recall from Chapter 2, we saw that when the marginal benefit of

some activity exceeded the _____ _____ , it paid to increase that activity. In the example, therefore, as long as the marginal

benefit to the farmer (the _____ _____ of labor input) exceeds the marginal cost to the farmer (the marginal wage rate), it will pay the farmer to continue hiring labor inputs.

5.26

Because the wage rate is constant and equal to 30 bushels, the farmer will not hire additional labor input whose marginal product is _(less/more)_ than 30 bushels. That is, if the marginal benefit to the farmer of an additional unit of

labor input (its marginal product) is less than the _____ _____ (the wage rate), that labor unit will not be hired.

5.27

Consider Figure 5.1, which is drawn from columns 1 and 4 in Table 5.1. It is very similar to the figures in Chapter 2. We can see that the first unit of

labor input adds _____ bushels to total output and the second

Answers

23. yes · no
24. 30 · marginal product
25. marginal cost · marginal product
26. less · marginal cost
27. 40

unit, _____ bushels. How much does the fifth unit add?

_____ bushels. You can see that after four units of labor input,

_____ returns set in.

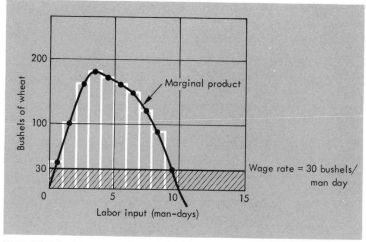

FIGURE 5.1 Marginal product of labor

5.28

Now, one way we could find out how much output five man-days would produce would be to add the output from the first man-day to the output from the second man-day, plus the third, fourth, and fifth. In terms of the

rectangles in Figure 5.1, we would add the _____ of the first five rectangles from the origin 0.

5.29

The sum of the areas of the first five rectangles, of course, is an approxima-

tion of the area under the _____ _____ curve from zero to five on the horizontal axis.

5.30

Similarly, the area under the _____ _____ curve between zero and nine units of labor input is total output (or total benefits to the farmer) from using nine units of labor input.

Answers

27. 100 · 170 · diminishing
28. areas
29. marginal product
30. marginal product

5.31

Now, consider the labor costs of producing output. Each man-day costs

_____ bushels and is shown by the horizontal wage line. The
line is horizontal because the cost of hiring an additional man does not
change as the amount of labor input changes. In other words, the marginal

_____ of labor input is constant.

5.32

The area under the _____ _____ curve from 0 to 15

on the horizontal axis represents the total _____ of labor to the
wheat farmer of employing 15 man-days; that is, this area represents

_____ bushels of wheat.

5.33

We can obtain, therefore, much useful information from Figure 5.1 because

the area under the _____ _____ of labor curve
represents total output (or total benefit) from hiring some given number of
labor inputs and because the area under the wage line represents the total

_____ of hiring some given number of labor inputs.

5.34

As long as the marginal product curve lies _(above/below)_ the wage line, the
last unit of labor hired will be yielding a return greater than its cost; that is,
the marginal benefit to the farmer of hiring that unit of labor will exceed

the _____ _____ .

5.35

If we continue to assume our farmer is a profit maximizer, he will not hire

an additional unit of labor input when the _____ benefit is less
than $30. Why? The benefit to the farmer in selling an additional bushel of
wheat is the extra money or marginal revenue he receives. Because the

Answers

31. 30 · cost
32. marginal cost · cost · 450
33. marginal product · cost
34. above · marginal cost
35. marginal

marginal revenue of selling an additional bushel of wheat is $1, the marginal benefit the farmer receives by hiring one additional unit of labor equals the

marginal revenue of wheat ($1) times the _____ _____ of labor. Thus, the farmer will only hire additional labor if the marginal revenue times the marginal product, that is, the marginal revenue product of

of labor, exceeds its _____ _____ .

5.36
We can generalize this simple example to include any factor input. Profit maximization requires that factor inputs are hired up to the point at which

the marginal _____ product of each factor input equals its

marginal _____ . In Figure 5.1, this means hiring up to 9½ man-days because at that level of labor input the marginal revenue product

of labor equals its _____ _____ equals $30.

5.37
Let us now assume, more realistically, that there are costs in addition to labor costs. If the farmer rents a 10 acre field for one year at $10 per acre, then, independent of how much wheat the farmer produces, he will have to

pay $ _____ in rent. This is a fixed cost of production because it _(will/will not)_ vary with the annual wheat output from this field.

5.38
If the farmer has to pay $30, however, for each man-day of labor employed, the amount of wages he must pay _(will/will not)_ vary with the number of units of labor input hired. These costs are known as variable costs. In this

example, they vary with the number of units of _____ _____ hired, and hence with the output of wheat.

5.39
We see from Table 5.1 that, up to the point of negative marginal product of

labor input, in order to obtain more wheat, we had to hire _____ units of labor input, and because this hiring necessarily involves paying more

Answers

    35.   marginal product · marginal cost
    36.   revenue · cost · marginal cost
    37.   100 · will not
    38.   will · labor input
    39.   more

wages, variable costs will indeed vary with total _____ of wheat.

Variable costs *(decrease/increase)* as total _____ increases up to
the maximum of 1,200 bushels when _____ units of labor input
are hired.

5.40

Turn now to Table 5.2, derived from data in Table 5.1. If we compare the

first two columns, we can see that _____ _____

_____ are independent of the annual output of wheat. This is
what we would expect because if the farmer commits himself to rent a 10
acre field at $10 per acre, this cost will be the same, regardless of his output of

wheat, consequently, we regard it as a _____ cost.

Table 5.2

FIXED, VARIABLE, AND TOTAL COSTS IN THE PRODUCTION OF WHEAT

(1) Annual output of wheat	(2) Total fixed costs	(3) Units of labor input (man-days)	(4) Total variable costs	(5) Total costs
0	$100	0	0	$100
40	100	1	30	130
140	100	2	60	160
300	100	3	90	190
480	100	4	120	220
650	100	5	150	250
810	100	6	180	280
960	100	7	210	310
1,080	100	8	240	340
1,170	100	9	270	370
1,200	100	10	300	400

5.41

The figures in columns 1 and 3 indicate how many units of labor input are
required to produce the various quantities of wheat. We also see that in order
to produce more wheat, we have to hire *(more/fewer)* units of labor input.

Answers

39.   output · increase · output · ten
40.   total fixed costs · fixed
41.   more

5.42

Because labor is our only variable input under our simplifying assumptions, the only factor input that will vary in quantity with total output will be

_____ input. Because we know the price or wage the farmer must pay for one man-day, we can calculate the labor costs corresponding to any given level of output. For instance, we see that in order to produce 650

bushels of wheat, we require _____ units of labor input. Thus,

the cost to the farmer of this labor input will be $ _____ .

5.43

Similarly, the labor costs to the farmer of producing 1,080 bushels of wheat

would be $ _____ , because this requires _____
units of labor input at $30 per man-day.

5.44

Thus, we can see how we derive the figures in column 4, which is headed *Total variable costs*. We derive those figures by multiplying the figures in

column _____ by $30—the cost of one unit of _____

input. Because the cost per unit of labor is constant and because a _____ quantity of labor input is required to produce a larger quantity of output, we would expect total variable costs to vary in the _(same/opposite)_ direction as total output.

5.45

We derive total cost by adding total fixed cost and _____ _____

_____ , and we find, as you would expect, that total cost varies in

the _____ direction as output.

5.46

In Figure 5.2, we have plotted the data in Table 5.2, and, as you would expect, the total fixed costs are represented by a horizontal line, because they do not

Answers

42. labor · five · 150
43. 240 · eight
44. 3 · labor · larger · same
45. total variable cost · same

_____ with the level of output. The total cost curve is derived by

adding the _____ _____ _____ curve to

the _____ _____ _____ curve.

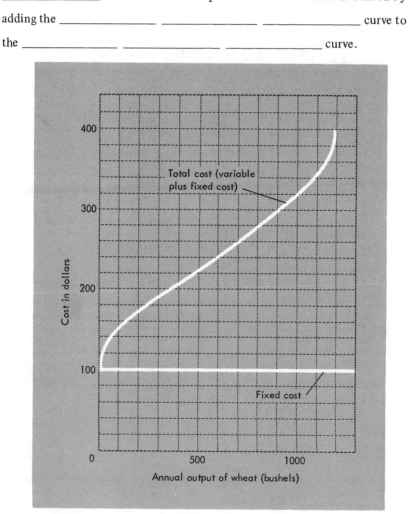

FIGURE 5.2   Fixed, variable, and total costs of production

5.47

In Table 5.3, data from Table 5.2 are repeated with some additional calcula-
tions. Average fixed costs are found by dividing total fixed costs by output;

similarly, average variable costs are calculated by dividing _____

Answers

46.   vary · total fixed cost · total variable cost
47.   total variable costs

_____ _____ by _____ and average

total costs, by dividing _____ _____ by output.

Table 5.3

TOTAL, AVERAGE, AND MARGINAL COSTS OF WHEAT PRODUCTION

(1) Output	(2) Total fixed costs	(3) Average fixed costs	(5) Total variable costs	(5) Average variable costs	(6) Total costs	(7) Average total costs	(8) Marginal cost
0	100	—	0	—	100	—	$0.75
40	100	$2.50	30	$0.75	130	$3.25	.30
140	100	.71	60	.43	160	1.14	.19
300	100	.33	90	.30	190	.63	.17
480	100	.21	120	.25	220	.46	.18
650	100	.15	150	.23	250	.38	.19
810	100	.12	180	.22	280	.35	.20
960	100	.10	210	.219	310	.32	.25
1,080	100	.09	240	.22	340	.31	.33
1,170	100	.085	270	.23	370	.32	1.00
1,200	100	.083	300	.25	400	.33	

5.48

Because total costs equal total fixed costs plus total _____

_____ , average total costs will equal average _____

_____ plus _____ variable costs.

5.49

The calculation of marginal cost is slightly more complex. Ideally, we want
to know the cost of producing one additional unit of output. We know, for
instance, that the total cost of producing 40 bushels of wheat is $130 and
the total cost of producing 140 bushels is $160. Thus, the difference in cost

of $ _____ is the marginal cost of producing an additional 100
bushels (that is, 140 − 40 bushels). If we treat each of those extra 100
bushels equally, we would calculate the marginal cost of one bushel as

$30/100 = $_____ .

Answers

47. output · total costs
48. variable costs · fixed costs · average
49. 30 · .30

5.50

The problem we are encountering here is the same one we discussed earlier in the book. We are not making continuous changes but rather discrete changes; not plotting the marginal and average curves for every atom of output but rather considering output in "lumps." The smooth curves are drawn through those lumps as though we had considered continuous changes. O.K.?

_____

5.51

We have plotted the average and marginal curves from Table 5.3 in Figure 5.3. To avoid having too messy a figure, we have omitted the average fixed cost curve that, if included, would be a line of _(constant/increasing/decreasing)_ height and that would measure the distance between the average total cost

curve and the _____   _____   _____ curve.

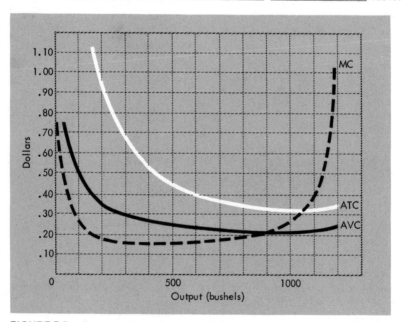

FIGURE 5.3   Average and marginal cost of wheat

Answers

   50. O.K.

   51. decreasing · average variable cost

5.52

Although we derive the marginal cost curve in Table 5.3 from total cost

figures, we could also derive the marginal cost from total _____
cost figures, because the marginal cost of producing additional wheat will be

independent of the _____   _____ .

5.53

Note two significant points in Figure 5.3. These are where the marginal cost
curve intersects the average variable cost curve and the average total cost
curve. In both instances, the marginal cost curve intersects each curve at its
(minimum/maximum) point. This is no accident but is necessarily true. We
can see from Figure 5.3 that as the marginal cost of producing additional
wheat equals the average total cost, the marginal cost curve must intersect

the average total cost curve at its _____ point, because once it
has intersected the average cost curve (and once marginal costs exceed

average costs), it will cause average total cost to _____ .

5.54

Think about a basketball squad. If the height of a sixth player is greater than
the average height of the other five, then the addition of this sixth man will

cause the average height to _____ .

5.55

To show in our example the exact relationships between the productivity of
labor input and the cost of wheat output, we shall pull together the tables
and figures we have analyzed in this chapter. From Table 5.1, we have
drawn total, average, and marginal product curves and alongside have reproduced the corresponding cost table and curves. You should work through
some numbers from each table and make sure you understand how each
curve is derived. For example, when marginal product becomes negative at

Answers

52. variable · fixed costs
53. minimum · minimum · rise
54. rise

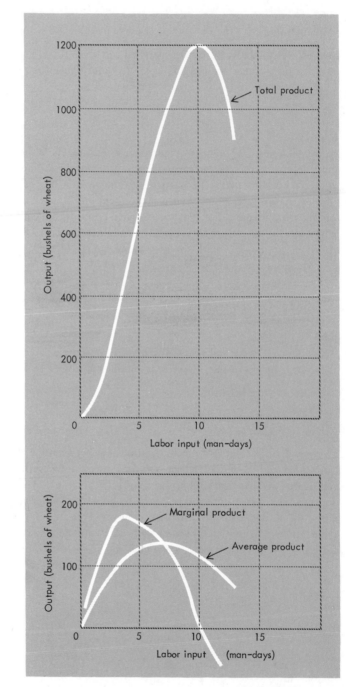

FIGURE 5.4
Total product
of labor

FIGURE 5.5
Marginal and
average product
of labor

10 man-days, you know that adding 1 more man-day will cause _____

_____ to fall. As can be seen, the total product curve is at a
maximum at 10 man-days.

5.56
By juxtaposing those figures into Figure 5.4, we see the relationship between
product and cost curves. The average variable cost curve will be inversely
related to the average product of labor curve, remembering that the wage per
man-day is set in the market and is constant. Thus, when the average product

per man-day is rising, average variable cost will be _____ , and
when average product per man-day is falling, average variable cost per unit of

output will be _____ .

5.57
Another way to express the same idea would be to say that the greater the
average product of each man-day of labor, the *(higher/lower)* the average
variable cost of each bushel of wheat produced. And, conversely, the less
wheat a man-day of labor can produce, the *(higher/lower)* the average
variable cost of each unit of wheat will be.

5.58
In Figure 5.6, a broken line traces the points we have discussed. We have

shown how the maximum _____ _____ point is

reflected at the _____ average variable cost point.

5.59
Just as the maximum value of the average product of labor yields the minimum

_____ _____ _____ , so the maximum

value of the marginal product of labor yields the _____ _____

_____ , as you can see from the other connecting lines in Figure
5.6.

Answers
55. total product
56. falling · rising
57. lower · higher
58. average product · minimum
59. average variable cost · minimum marginal cost

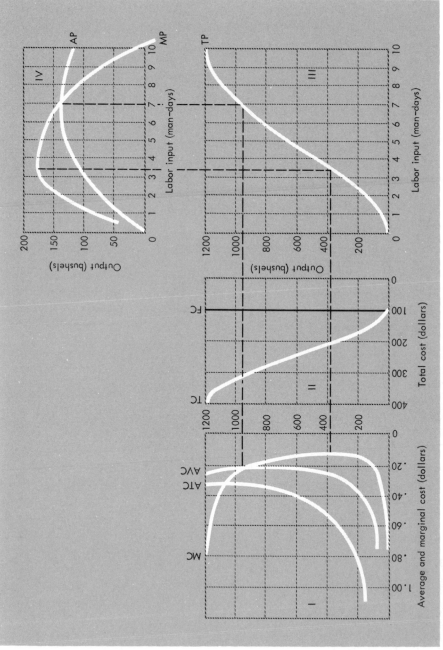

FIGURE 5.6 The relationship between productivity and cost

5.60

We have just seen how the profit-maximizing farmer in our simple example
hired labor up to the point at which the marginal benefit to him, that is, the

marginal revenue product of labor, just equalled the _____

_____ to him, that is, the wage or price of the last unit of labor
hired.

5.61

There are important implications in this statement not only for the competitive firm, which we shall study in Chapter 6, but also for the returns to
factors of production, particularly labor (or people), which we shall study in
Chapter 12. If each worker is paid the value of his _____

_____ , and for most people the primary source of income is
derived from the sale of their labor services, how well off a person is will
depend upon what his contribution is to total output. Individuals whose
marginal products are low—the unskilled—tend to have very low incomes. As
we shall see, understanding the reasons for those different marginal productivi-
ties helps to explain the reason for widely different levels of income and
standards of living within the U.S. and among different peoples of the world.

REVIEW QUESTIONS

5.1

Which of the following cannot increase, other things being equal, as output
increases?

a. average total cost
b. average variable cost
c. average fixed cost
d. marginal cost

Fixed cost is independent of the level of output. If a farmer rents a field for
$500 for a year, he must pay this cost whether he produces any output or
not. Average fixed cost for the farmer will equal $500 divided by output and,

Answers
    60.   marginal cost
    61.   marginal product

consequently, the larger the output, the smaller the average fixed cost. Average total cost, average variable cost, and marginal cost typically decrease and, after some level of output, increase. The correct response is c.

5.2

If a firm is producing output at a point where diminishing returns have set in, which of the following is correct?

1. Each additional unit of output will be more expensive to produce.
2. Each additional unit of output will require increasing amounts of the factor of production being increased.
3. The marginal product of the variable factor of production decreases as the quantity used increases.

    a. 1 only
    b. 1 and 2 only
    c. 2 and 3 only
    d. 1, 2, and 3

Diminishing returns means that the amount of additional output obtained through adding an extra unit of one factor input, holding the amount of other factors fixed, will decrease as the level of output increases. That is, the marginal product of the variable factor input must be falling. This means that to produce one more unit of output, the higher the level of output, the greater the additional amount required to make an extra unit of output. Consequently, each additional unit of output will be more expensive to produce. The correct response is d.

5.3

Questions 5.3 and 5.4 are based on the following data, which are for a tomato farmer who can hire tomato pickers at $12 per day:
    The profit maximizing farmer should hire only

a. One tomato picker because his contribution to output is greatest.
b. Three tomato pickers because the fourth costs more than he earns.
c. Eight tomato pickers because costs will equal revenue.
d. Nine tomato pickers because the value of the marginal product of the tenth picker is zero.

The rule for profit maximization is that factor inputs be hired up to the point at which the value of the marginal product equals the price of the factor input. In the example, the price of the factor input, the tomato picker, is $12. We can calculate the value of the marginal product of each tomato picker by

simple subtraction in column 2. For example, the value of the marginal
product of the first picker is $30. The second picker increases the value of
output by $18 ($48 - $30), and the third, by $14 ($62 - $48). The fourth,
however, adds only $10 to the value of output ($72 - $62), and because he
costs $12, the farmer would lose $2 by hiring him. Thus, he will not hire a
fourth picker. The correct response is b.

Number of pickers	Tomato output
1	$30
2	48
3	62
4	72
5	80
6	87
7	93
8	96
9	98
10	98

5.4
The local authorities, in an attempt to make the tomato pickers better off,
legislate that tomato pickers must be paid a wage no less than $16 per day. If
our profit-maximizing farmer complies, which of the following will be
correct?

1. Each of the three tomato pickers our farmer had previously hired will become better off.
2. The value of the average product of labor will fall.
3. The quantity of tomato output will fall.

   a. 1 only
   b. 2 and 3 only
   c. 3 only
   d. 1, 2, and 3

Again, our profit-maximizing farmer will hire labor to the point where the
value of the marginal product of labor equals the price of labor. However,
because the price of labor, or wage, has risen to $16, he will no longer hire
the third picker whose marginal product is only $14. Consequently, the two
pcikers retained will become better off; the third will become worse off.
Tomato output will fall. The value of the average product of labor, however,
will rise because $48/2 is greater than $62/3. The correct response is c.

6

Firm Supply

6.1

In Chapter 5, we analyzed how the productivity of factor inputs determined

the _____ of production at different output levels. We assumed
all factor inputs but one (labor, in our farming example) to be fixed. In this
chapter, the analysis will continue, and we shall show how the profit-maximizing competitive firm behaves—first when some factor inputs are fixed and
then when all are variable. Such analysis is necessary to understand not only how
the goods and services we consume daily are produced but also the many
interdependencies in our economic system.

6.2

You will recall from Chapter 5 that our farmer had certain fixed costs. He
rented a 10-acre field for $100 and paid this $100 *(dependent upon/independent*

 of) the level of output. His labor costs were _____ costs, however, because they varied with the level of output.

Answers
> 1.   costs
> 2.   independent of · variable

6.3

In this chapter, we are going to consider a firm in two different time periods; first in the *short run,* when some costs, like our farmer's field rental, are

_____ and independent of the level of output and second in the *long run* when no costs are fixed.

6.4

You cannot define the *short run* in terms of days or months because it varies from example to example. We define the *short run* to be that period within which some costs are fixed; fixed costs do not vary with changes in output.

The _____ run is that time period in which all costs can vary. Thus, at the expiration of the lease, when he was planning how much wheat

to grow the following year, he could vary the amount of _____ as well as the amount of labor, that is, *(no/some)*____ factor was fixed, independent of the planned output level. Once he rents a field, however, he is back

into a _____ run situation.

6.5

The reason for this short-run—long-run distinction will be clear by the end of this chapter. We shall first consider the competitive firm in the short run, and we shall assume that the aim of the firm is *profit maximization.* We wish to know what output a competitive firm should produce in the short run in

which certain costs are _____ , given that the firm's goal is to

maximize _____ .

6.6

The gross income a firm receives from the sale of its product is known as its revenue. Thus, if we use the jargon of economists, we would say that the total income received by a manufacturer from sales in some given time period (say

one month) is total _____ .

Answers
3. fixed
4. long · land · no · short
5. fixed · profit
6. revenue

6.7

When total revenue from some specific output exceeds the total cost of

producing that output, the firm will make a _____ at that level
of output. If, however, total costs are greater than total revenue for some
specific output, the firm will make a loss (that is, will have a negative

_____) at that level of output.

6.8

Let us consider Table 6.1, which shows total cost, total revenue, and profit
for a manufacturer of water beds.

Table 6.1

TOTAL COST, REVENUE, AND PROFIT

Output	Total cost	Total revenue	Profit
0	$ 270	$ 0	$−270
1	360	100	−260
2	410	200	−210
3	440	300	−140
4	460	400	− 60
5	470	500	30
6	500	600	100
7	560	700	140
8	660	800	140
9	830	900	70
10	1,110	1,000	−110

This manufacturer produces identical water beds and he can sell as many as he
can produce for $100 each. We derive the figures in the third column in Table

6.1 by multiplying $100 by the level of _____ . If the manufacturer
sells 10 water beds per month, the total revenue for that month would be

$ _____ . If he sells 4 beds, his total revenue will be $ _____,

and if he sells 0 beds, the total revenue will be $ _____ .

Answers

    7. profit · profit
    8. output · 1,000 · 400 · 0

6.9

Let us now consider the manufacturer's cost of production. When the manufacturer produces zero water beds the only cost incurred will be fixed cost. In this example, fixed cost, which is the same at all levels of output, equals

$ _____ . From the first and second columns, we see that total

cost (variable plus _____ cost) increases as output _____ .

6.10

We obtain the profit figures in the fourth column by subtracting total

_____ from total _____ . If, in some given month,
the manufacturer produces no water beds (perhaps everyone is having a

month's vacation), the only cost that will be incurred will be _____

cost but because total revenue will be $ _____ , profit will be

$ _____ .

6.11

We see that if the manufacturer produces one water bed per month, his loss

(negative profit) will be $ _____ . In fact, he makes losses if he

produces less than _____ water beds per month or more than

_____ .

6.12

It is only in the range of output of _____ to _____
water beds per month that the manufacturers will make positive profit. Given
that the aim of the manufacturer is to maximize profit, it is obvious from

Table 6.1 that he will produce either _____ or _____
water beds, because either of those outputs gives a maximum profit per month

of $ _____ .

Answers

9. 270 · fixed · increases
10. cost · revenue · fixed · 0 · −270
11. 260 · 5 · 9
12. 5 · 9 · 7 · 8 · 140

6.13

In Figure 6.1, we have plotted the data from Table 6.1. Because each water bed

sells for $ _____ , total revenue increases by $ _____
for each additional unit of output. As a result, total revenue is represented in

Figure 6.1 by a _____ line.

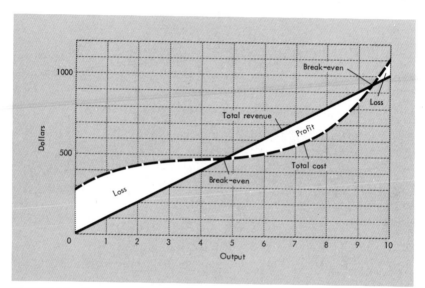

FIGURE 6.1   Revenue, cost, and profit

6.14

The total cost curve is shaped similarly to the total cost curves we have

already analyzed. We see that at 0 output, total cost is $ _____ .

At this level of output, total cost equals _____ cost. As output
increases, total cost increases fairly quickly at first, then more slowly for
levels of output between 2 and 7 and then fairly sharply again for higher
levels of output. We also see that our total cost curve intersects our total

revenue curve at levels of output of between _____ and

_____ and also 9 and 10. When this occurs, profit of course is

_____ ; the manufacturer is at a break-even point, making
neither profit nor loss.

Answers

13.   100 · 100 · straight
14.   270 · fixed · 4 · 5 · 0

6.15

For all levels of output less than five, total cost _____ total revenue and, consequently, profit is negative. This situation is similar for

levels of output greater than _____ beds per month where once more total cost exceeds total revenue.

6.16

For levels of output between five and nine water beds, _____

_____ exceeds _____ _____ , and,

consequently, _____ is positive.

6.17

The level of profit at the monthly output of five water beds could be found

by taking the vertical distance between the _____ _____

curve and the _____ _____ curve at a level of output

of five beds. This distance would be $30, which would be the _____ for that level of output.

6.18

Because our water bed manufacturer wishes to maximize profit, he will

choose that level of output where the distance between _____

_____ curve and the _____ _____

curve is a maximum.

6.19

Thus, our manufacturer will be maximizing _____ if he produces

either _____ or _____ water beds per month. In both

cases, profit will be $ _____ .

Answers

15. exceeds · 9
16. total revenue · total cost · profit
17. total revenue · total cost · profit
18. total revenue · total cost
19. profit · 7 · 8 · 140

6.20

Just as the distance between total revenue and total cost shows (positive)

_____ for outputs of five to nine water beds, so will this distance

show a _____ (negative profit) for levels of output less than five and greater than nine. Thus, given the range of outputs in Figure 6.1, maxi-

mum loss would be incurred at an output level of _____ water

beds per week, and would amount to $ _____ . The level of out-

put that would produce the second highest loss would be _____

water bed (s) per month, at which the extent of the loss would be $ _____ .

6.21

Given our knowledge of costs, there is a more useful way we can calculate the profit-maximizing output for our water bed manufacturer. Look at Table 6.2. In the third column, we have calculated marginal cost, which you will remember is the cost of producing an additional water bed. We see, for

instance, that the total cost of producing two water beds is $ _____ ,

and the total cost of producing one water bed is $ _____ . Thus, the cost of increasing production from one to two water beds is the difference between those two figures, which is $50. Thus, when output is one water bed

per month, _____ cost is $50.

Table 6.2

MARGINAL COST AND MARGINAL REVENUE

Output	Total cost	Marginal cost	Total revenue	Marginal revenue
0	$ 270		$ 0	
		$ 90		$100
1	360		100	
		50		100
2	410		200	
		30		100
3	440		300	
		20		100
4	460		400	
		10		100
5	470		500	
		30		100
6	500		600	
		60		100
7	560		700	
		100		100
8	660		800	
		170		100
9	830		900	
		280		100˙
10	1,110		1,000	

Answers

20. profit · loss · zero · 270 · one · 260
21. 410 · 360 · marginal

6.22
Similarly, the marginal cost of producing the fifth water bed is $ _____ .

This figure is derived by subtracting the cost of producing _____

water beds, which is $ _____ , from the cost of producing

_____ water beds, which is $ _____ .

6.23
In a similar fashion, we can calculate marginal revenue. Marginal revenue is

the additional revenue collected by selling one _____ water
bed. Because the selling price of each water bed is the same, the extra
revenue from selling an additional water bed is *(less than/equal to)* the
price. Thus, in this example, marginal revenue is a constant, equal to

$ _____ because price is equal to $ _____ .

6.24
Let us now see how our marginal cost and marginal revenue columns can
help us determine the profit-maximizing output. Suppose, for example, our
water bed firm is producing two units of output and wants to decide whether
to produce a third unit. You know from Table 6.2 that at two units of out-

put, the marginal revenue is $ _____ and the marginal cost is

$ _____ .

6.25
If, by producing an extra bed, revenue is increased by $100 and cost is in-
creased by $30, would the change be worthwhile? The answer to this ques-
tion is *(yes/no)* because such a change would *(increase/decrease)* profit

(or decrease loss) by $ _____ .

6.26
Thus, you can see that it will always pay to produce an extra unit of output
as long as the marginal revenue (that is, the marginal benefit to the water bed
manufacturer) of an extra unit is *(greater/less)* than the marginal cost.

Answers
22. 10 · 4 · 460 · 5 · 470
23. additional · equal to · 100 · 100
24. 100 · 30
25. yes · increase · 70
26. greater

6.27

At what level of output will there be no gain from producing an extra unit?

_____ units. It is here that _____ revenue and

_____ cost are equal and _____ is a maximum.

6.28

The extra cost incurred in producing the seventh water bed is _____
than the extra revenue received from its sale. Thus, it is profitable to produce
the seventh water bed. The marginal cost of producing an eighth water bed is

$ _____ , and the marginal revenue from its sale is $ _____ .
Thus, we would say that the manufacturer would be indifferent (he would not
care from the viewpoint of maximizing profit) as to whether or not he produced and sold this eighth water bed. He would not, however, produce more
than eight water beds because that would take him beyond the point at which

_____ _____ equals marginal cost.

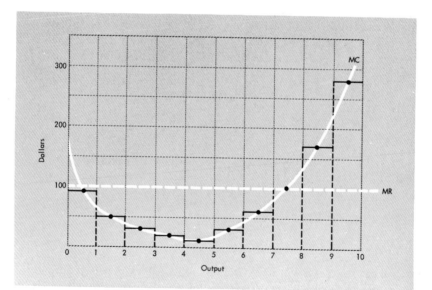

FIGURE 6.2 Marginal cost and marginal revenue

6.29

With the help of one of our earlier diagrams, we can briefly summarize the
foregoing analysis. Adding the 10 rectangles in Figure 6.2 would yield the

total _____ cost of 10 water beds.

6.30

Using the continuous curve (the MC curve) instead, we know that the

_____ under the curve also measures the _____

_____ of 10 water beds.

6.31

The area under the MR curve between 0 and 10 equals the _____

_____ from selling 10 water beds. This area represents $ _____ .

6.32

Thus, ignoring fixed cost for the moment, as long as the area under the MR curve

is _____ than the area under the MC curve, profit will be positive.
However, as soon as the MC curve lies above the MR curve, the benefits

(revenue) from producing additional water beds are _____
than the costs of those additional water beds. Consequently, the profit-maximizing entrepreneur will not produce beyond the point where MR =

_____ .

6.33

You should note that it is a necessary condition for profit maximization

that _____ _____ equal _____

_____ ; but this is not a sufficient condition. MC must also be
rising. For example, the MC curve intersects the MR curve between output
levels of 0 and 1, but this is not a profit-maximizing output level because the

_____ curve is falling.

Answers

29. variable
30. area · variable cost
31. total revenue · 1,000
32. greater · less · MC
33. marginal revenue (MR) · marginal cost (MC) · MC

6.34

Thus, we can summarize what we have learned in Figure 6.2 by saying that a profit-seeking entrepreneur will increase output up to that point at which marginal revenue equals marginal cost. It will not pay him to stop before that point is reached because the marginal revenue collected from each additional water bed exceeds the _____ _____ of producing that water bed. _____ will not be maximized by producing beyond the point at which marginal revenue equals marginal cost, because the marginal revenue collected from sales of additional water beds will be _____ than the marginal cost of producing them.

6.35

Thus, as long as producing and selling additional water beds adds more to total revenue than it does to total cost, it will pay the manufacturer to do so. This statement is the same as saying that a profit-seeking manufacturer should increase his output up to that point at which marginal revenue equals

_____ _____ .

6.36

We derived total revenue by multiplying the selling price of each water bed ($100) by the number of units produced. If we wish to calculate average revenue figures from total revenue figures, we reverse the process, that is, we divide total revenue by output. In our water bed example, we would, of course, obtain a figure of $ _____ as the average revenue for each level of output. Because each additional water bed sold yields $100, the _____ revenue for each level of output must also be $100.

6.37

In Figure 6.3, we have plotted selling price, average revenue, and marginal revenue against output, with the prices on the vertical axis and output on the horizontal axis. We have one horizontal line crossing the vertical axis at a price of $ _____ , representing all three. This line is also the demand curve facing the manufacturer. This demand curve shows that the

Answers

34. marginal cost · Profit · less
35. marginal cost
36. 100 · marginal
37. 100

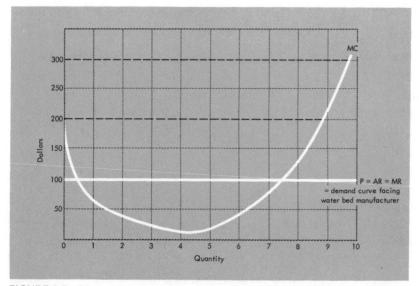

FIGURE 6.3   Price, marginal revenue, and marginal cost

water bed manufacturer can sell as many water beds as he wants at a price of
$100 each. It also tells us that the number of water beds our manufacturer

can sell at any price greater than $100 is _____ , because
potential water bed customers can buy identical water beds at $100 from a
competitor on the next block. Because one manufacturer can sell as many
water beds as he wishes at $100, but none at a price greater than $100, it
_(will/will never)_____ be in his interests to charge a lower price.

6.38
If the going price of water beds were $200 each rather than $100, how
would our manufacturer react? He would be faced with _(a new/the same)_____
demand curve, _(a new/the same)_P = AR = MR curve, and _(a new/the same)_
MC curve.

6.39
Because his goal is _____ maximization, he will produce water

beds up to the point at which MR = _____ .

Answers
>   37.   0 ·   will never
>   38.   a new · a new · the same
>   39.   profit · MC

6.40

Because the price of water beds is now $200, marginal revenue will now equal

$ _____ . The new MR curve intersects the MC curve at an out-

put level of between _____ and _____ water beds.

6.41

Similarly, if the price were $300 per water bed, our manufacturer would pro-

duce between _____ and _____ water beds per
month.

6.42

Because the marginal cost curve of our manufacturer tells us how many water
beds he would produce each month at any price, the MC is in reality the
firm's monthly _(demand/supply)_ curve. From Figure 6.3, we have learned
that between 7 and 8 water beds would be produced monthly if the price

were $ _____ and between 9 and 10 if the price were

$ _____ .

6.43

In the example just discussed, the firm's revenue exceeded its variable costs,

and its short-run supply curve is its _____ _____
curve. If at the going price of water beds, however, the firm were not receiving sufficient revenue to cover the costs of labor and raw materials, it
would lose more than just its fixed cost. If the firm were to shut down and

produce nothing, its losses would equal just its _____ cost. In
such a case, it would pay the firm to _(shut down/continue to produce)_ because
that would minimize its losses.

6.44

Let us summarize our findings. To have a profitable level of output, _____

_____ must exceed total cost.

Answers

40. 200 · 9 · 10
41. 9 · 10
42. supply · 100 · 300
43. marginal cost · fixed · shut down
44. total revenue

6.45

When total cost equals _____ _____ , we have a

break-even level of output, that is, our manufacturer makes neither a _____

nor a _____ at that output level.

6.46

In the short-run, the loss incurred by a manufacturer from closing down will

equal his _____ _____ . From a _____-
minimizing viewpoint, this closing down would be rational behavior if there
is no level of output that will yield sufficient revenue to at least cover

_____ _____ .

6.47

In the short run, that time period when some costs are fixed, the equilibrium

output of the firm will be that output at which _____ _____

equals _____ _____ . In this short run, other levels of
output may yield a profit, but not a maximum profit.

6.48

In the short run, therefore, once the firm has reached that _____
position, profit cannot be increased by altering the output level. The short-

run supply curve of the firm is its _____ _____ curve
for all outputs where variable costs have been met.

6.49

In the real world, consumers' tastes and preferences are constantly changing,
new goods and services come into being, research and development discover
new uses for natural resources, and technological change is constantly occurring.
Because of all this, we would be very surprised if firms ever settled for long, or
even reached a long-run equilibrium position, that is, a position from which
there would be no incentive to change. However, although firms may never

reach a long-run _____ position from which there is no incentive

Answers

45. total revenue · profit · loss
46. fixed cost · loss · variable cost
47. marginal revenue · marginal cost
48. equilibrium · marginal cost
49. equilibrium

to change, we define *long-run equilibrium* as a position toward which firms move and that would ultimately be reached, in the absence of any other changes. Thus, long-run equilibrium is an abstract concept. It is a position toward which firms would move, were other things to *(remain the same/change)* .

6.50

In Chapter 1, we recognized that whenever a choice is made we must give

up one of the alternatives; that is, we have to accept the _____ cost. Thus, there is a cost to produce a commodity that is over and above the costs that have to be paid out as wages, rent, and so on. This cost is the profit that could be earned by using resources in the best alternative use; it is the entrepreneur's opportunity cost. In our example, the profit that the water bed manufacturer could earn if he produced conventional furni-

ture instead of water beds is his _____ _____ .

6.51

In the long run, in our example, if our water bed manufacturer does not

earn enough profit to cover his _____ cost, he will shift his resources to the production of conventional furniture. We can say the same thing a different way. If an entrepreneur cannot earn as much profit in the production of good A as he can in the production of good B, then in the

_____ _____ he will shift to the production of good B.

6.52

If our water bed manufacturer cannot cover his opportunity cost in the production of water beds, it means that he can earn a *(higher/lower)* profit in the production of some other commodity, and in the long run will shift his resources from the production of water beds to the production of that commodity for which the return is highest. Remember, we are assuming he wants the highest return possible.

6.53

In our diagrams, we have included the entrepreneur's opportunity cost as one of the fixed costs of production. Thus, in these diagrams, when a firm

Answers
49. remain the same
50. opportunity · opportunity cost
51. opportunity · long run
52. higher

is earning a profit, it means that it is earning a profit that is _(greater/less)_
than the profit that could be earned by taking advantage of any alternative
opportunity.

6.54
In other words, in our diagrams, when a firm is earning a profit, it means
that is is earning enough profit to discourage it from shifting resources to
the production of a different commodity. Is this statement true or false?

_____

6.55
Thus, if a firm is producing so that total cost equals total revenue, we say
that the firm is earning a normal profit. By this we mean that its revenue is

just enough to cover all costs including its _____ cost, but is not
earning any profit in excess of what is required to keep the firm in that line
of production.

6.56
Consider now the behavior of our water bed manufacturer in the long run.
Because no factors of production are fixed in the long run, it _(is/is not)_
possible for the manufacturer to increase or decrease the scale of his opera-
tions by acquiring a new workshop, larger or smaller store, larger or smaller
manufacturing equipment, as well as changing the amount of labor he hires.
In the short run, the firm _(can/cannot)_ change its output, but only by
increasing or decreasing the factors of production that are _____
in the short run.

6.57
The rule that the water bed manufacturer used for _____
maximization in the short run will be used for profit maximization in the long
run with one important modification. That modification is that marginal
revenue must equal _long-run_ marginal cost.

Answers
53. greater
54. true
55. opportunity
56. is · can · variable
57. profit

6.58

The logic is the same as that which we adopted in analyzing short-run, profit-maximizing behavior. Consider Figure 6.4.

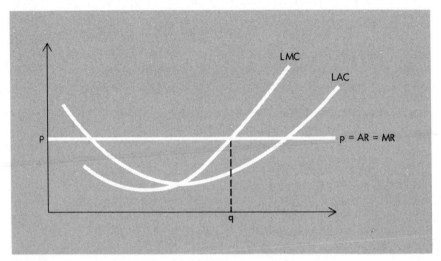

FIGURE 6.4   Long-run equilibrium of the firm

For outputs less than q, the benefit to our manufacturer from selling one more water bed, that is, that ___(MR/LMC)___ , exceeds the cost to him of producing it when all factors are variable, that is, the _____ .

6.59

Similarly, in the long run for output levels greater than q, MR is less than

_____ and, consequently, the production of an additional bed

adds more to _____ than it does to revenue, which means that

_____ will be reduced.

6.60

The desire to maximize profit, therefore, will indicate to our water bed manufacturer that in the long run he produces that number of water beds

for which marginal revenue equals _____ - _____

_____ _____ .

Answers

    58.   MR · LMC
    59.   LMC · cost · profit
    60.   long-run marginal cost (LMC)

6.61

It will also tell him what size of plant or factory or store he should have. He

should incur those fixed costs that yield an output for which _____

_____ equals long-run marginal cost.

6.62

For example, if we superimpose this optimally sized plant on our long-run
equilibrium diagram, we would have Figure 6.5.

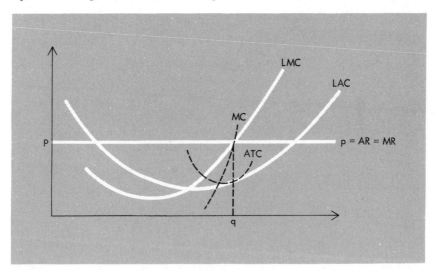

FIGURE 6.5   Long-run equilibrium of the firm

Here we can see that the firm is in both _____ - _____

and _____ - _____ equilibrium.

6.63

In other words, for output q in Figure 6.5, any other plant size (incurring
any other set of fixed costs) would give a *(higher/lower)* average total cost
than the plant drawn. In other words, our manufacturer would not be on
his LAC. Thus, for price p, no other plant size would allow MR to equal

LMC and consequently maximize _____ .

Answers
    61.   marginal revenue
    62.   short-run · long-run (either order)
    63.   higher · profit

6.64

Of course, once our manufacturer has decided on his optimally sized plant

and has incurred the accompanying _____ costs, he will be back
in a short-run situation. If price changes, he will maximize short-run profit

by producing that output for which _____ _____

equals short-run _____ _____ . Only if price and
the state of technology of water bed making and other factors do not

change will he be in both _____ - _____ and

_____ - _____ equilibrium. Long-run equilibrium,
however, despite all the uncertainties in real life, is the position he will aim
for even though he may never actually attain it.

6.65

Because price is equal to marginal revenue for our firm, it will expand output to the level at which price is equal to the long-run marginal cost. Consequently, the long-run supply curve of the firm will be the long-run

_____ _____ curve above the minimum point of
the LAC, which is where those curves intersect.

6.66

Why, in the long-run, will the firm supply zero output if p is less than LAC?

The reason is simple; the firm would not make a _____ ;
resources could be used more profitably in some other activity because

_____ costs would not be covered.

6.67

So far, we have considered the firm in the short run, when some costs are

fixed, and in the long run, when all _____ are _____ .
We have derived the firm's short-run supply curve, which tells us what output a firm would supply, given its fixed costs, at different prices. We also
derived the firm's long-run supply curve, which again tells us what output

Answers

64. fixed · marginal revenue · marginal cost · short-run ·
long-run (either order)
65. marginal cost
66. profit · opportunity (total)
67. costs · variable

the firm would supply at different _____ when no fixed costs had been incurred.

6.68

The firm's supply curves, short-run and long-run, are similar to a demand curve in the sense that it involves a "would" - "if" proposition. The firm's supply curves represent hypothetical situations telling us what the firm

_____ produce _____ certain prices ruled, other things unchanged. As we shall see in Chapter 8, price is determined by the forces of market demand and market supply. We shall now proceed from firm to market supply in Chapter 7.

REVIEW QUESTIONS

6.1

Suppose that on the day before Christmas, the local florist has a number of cut Christmas trees for sale that he will throw away (at no cost to himself) if they are not sold that day. Each tree cost the florist $3. What price should he set if he wants to maximize profit?

a. A price that gives the greatest profit per tree sold.
b. A price just low enough to make sure that all trees will be sold.
c. A price that maximizes total receipts (that is, price x quantity sold).
d. A price greater than his cost of $3.

Fixed costs are fixed costs and in the short run should not influence the florist in selling his Christmas trees. The fact that he has paid $3 per tree is irrelevant to the profit-maximizing (loss-minimizing) decision. Because disposal costs of unsold trees are zero, the florist must attempt to obtain as large a total revenue as possible from the sale of trees, that is, make price times quantity sold a maximum. Thus, the set price need not guarantee either that all trees be sold or that the $3 purchase price be recovered. The correct response is c.

Questions 2, 3, and 4 are based on the following data:

At its present level of output of 400 units, a perfectly competitive firm discovers that its marginal cost is $4. At an output level of 300 units, marginal

Answers

67. prices
68. would · if

cost is $3 and is equal to average total cost. The price of the commodity being produced is $5.

6.2

If the firm wishes to maximize profit, which of the following should it do?

a. increase output
b. decrease output
c. raise price
d. lower price

In answering the question, it might help you to draw a diagram. Because the firm is perfectly competitive, the demand curve facing it is represented by a horizontal line. The line also represents price = $5 = average revenue = marginal revenue. Certain points on the marginal cost curve can be plotted. At an output level of 300 units, MC = $3 (and at that point average total cost is at a minimum because MC intersects ATC at its minimum point), and at an output level of 400 units, MC = $4. Let us plot these points and lines.

By projecting the MC curve (given it does not rise vertically at an output level of 400 units), we see that MC intersects MR at an output level greater than 400 units. Thus, to maximize profit, the firm should increase output. It should not change its price, first because it will not be able to sell any output at a price greater than $5 and second because it can sell as much as it can produce at $5—there is no incentive to decrease price. The correct response is a.

6.3

At the present level of output, how much does the four-hundredth unit of output add to profit?

a. $5
b. $4
c. $3
d. $1

Using our diagram, in Figure 6.2a, we see that the MC of the four-hundredth unit is $4 and MR equals $5. The difference of $1 is what the four-hundredth unit adds to profit. The correct response is d.

6.4

The firm will be in equilibrium in the short-run when:

1. it is maximizing profit.
2. MC = $5.
3. minimum ATC = $5.

Which of the above is correct?

a. 1 only
b. 1 and 2 only
c. 1 and 3 only
d. 1, 2, and 3

Again using our diagram, the firm will maximize profit in the short run when
MR = MC = $5. In the long run, as resources move into the industry in
response to the excess profit, the AR = MR curve will fall. The correct response is b.

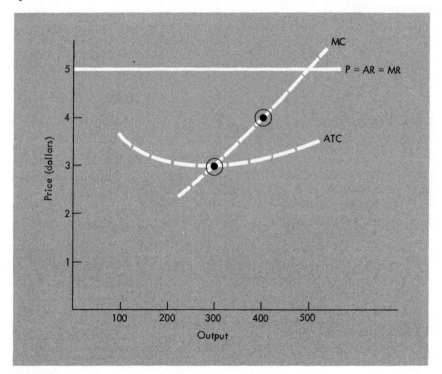

FIGURE 6.2a   Non-profit maximizing firm

7

Market Supply

7.1
Just as we assumed when discussing the consumer that no single individual was a significant force affecting prices and output in competitive markets, so we shall make the same assumption for firms as suppliers in these markets. In other words, our water bed manufacturer producing six or seven or eight water beds per month *(does/does not)* significantly affect the price of water beds. His production is an insignificant part of total production. All water bed manufacturers taken together in some market, however, will have a significant impact on price.

7.2
In Figure 7.1, consider three water bed manufacturers, A, B, and C producing identical products. Assume the going price of a water bed is $100. How many

beds will A product? _____ . Quite correct, he will produce 10 beds because at this output the benefit to A of producing the tenth bed, that is, the

_____ _____ , just equals the marginal cost.

Answers
1. does not
2. 10 · marginal revenue

130

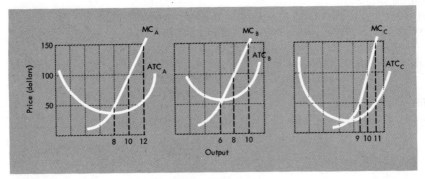

FIGURE 7.1   Cost curves for three different firms

7.3

Similarly, in order to maximize short-run _____ , B and C will

produce _____ and _____ beds per month respec-

tively. If the price per water bed were $150 instead of $100, how many

water beds would each produce? A—_____ : B—_____;

C—_____ . In similar fashion, we could repeat this process for

every possible price, asking how much each manufacturer would produce if a

certain price were to rule.

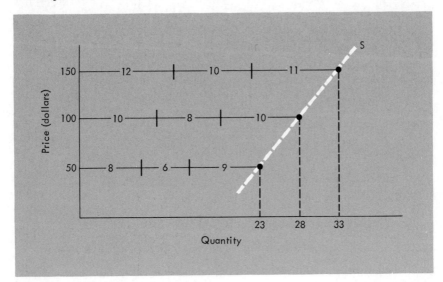

FIGURE 7.2   Market supply in the short-run

Answers

3. profit · 8 · 10 · 12 · 10 · 11

7.4
Figure 7.2 is derived from Figure 7.1 and shows the ___(firm/market)___ supply,
assuming the only suppliers are A, B, and C. For example, at a price of $150
per water bed, the total supplied by the three firms would be $12 + 10 + 11$,
which adds up to 33 beds.

7.5
Just as the short-run supply curve of the individual firm is its _____

_____ curve above the minimum point of its average variable cost
curve, so the aggregate supply curve S will be the summation of all the firms'

short-run supply curves, that is, a summation of their _____

_____ curves.

7.6
The relationship between the short-run market supply curve and the short-
run supply curve for a typical firm is shown in Figure 7.3.

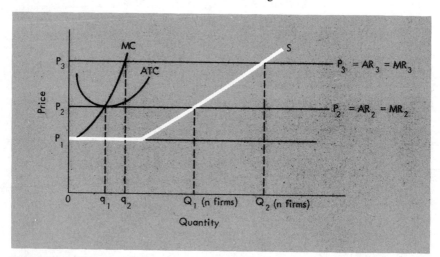

FIGURE 7.3   Firm and market supply in the short-run

At price P_2, the firm represented by ATC and MC would produce output

_____ . From the market supply curve S, we can see that the n

firms taken together would produce _____ .

Answers
   4.   market
   5.   marginal cost   ·   marginal cost
   6. $0q_1$ · $0Q_1$

7.7

Because market supply for prices below P_1 equals _____ , we

can conclude that no firm has an _____ _____

_____ curve whose minimum point is less than P_1.

7.8

At price of P_3, the individual firm in Figure 7.3 would produce _____ .

Why? Because at that output MR = _____ . The n firms taken

together would produce _____ .

7.9

In Figure 7.3, when the price is P_3, the firm will be making _____
over and above the opportunity cost of the resources employed, by producing that level of output at which P_3 (which is equal to AR and MR) =

_____ .

7.10

Now consider what will happen in the long run. Businessmen will observe

_____ being made by firms in the industry depicted in Figure
7.3 and, being profit motivated, will divert resources into the industry.

7.11

First, consider the case in which the movement of new firms into the industry
does not increase the prices of the factors of production employed in this

industry. Thus, the _____ of producing a unit of output will not
increase as new firms move in.

7.12

In the long run, new firms will continue to move into the industry as long as

_____ exists. Profit will exist as long as price is greater than the

Answers

7.	zero	·	average variable cost
8.	$0q_2$	· MC ·	$0Q_2$
9.	profit	·	MC
10.	profit		
11.	cost		
12.	profit		

average total cost of production; that is, as long as the _____ is above the minimum point of the average total cost curve.

7.13

In Figure 7.3, because firms would continue to enter the industry as long as price is greater than P_2, industry output would _____ for prices greater than P_2. Zero output would be supplied in the long run for prices below P_2, however, because for prices less than P_2, long-run average

_____ _____ of production will not be covered. Therefore, in this example, the long-run market (or industry) supply curve will be represented by a horizontal line at price P_2.

7.14

Remember, we are assuming here that the _____ of production does not increase as more firms move into the industry. The short-run industry supply curve, of course, will be a *(negatively inclined/horizontal/*

positively inclined)   line, but the long-run industry supply curve, a _____ line.

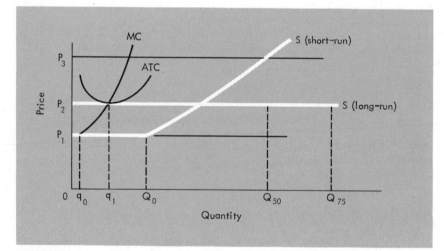

FIGURE 7.4   Long-run supply (constant cost)

Answers

   12.   price
   13.   increase · total cost
   14.   cost · positively inclined · horizontal

7.15

This can be seen in Figure 7.4. If there were 50 identical firms in the industry,

supply at a price of P_2 would be $0Q_{50}$. Each firm would produce _____ .
If there were 75 identical firms instead and the price were still P_2, total industry

supply would be _____ . Each firm still would produce $0q_1$.

7.16

For any price below P_2, firms would be unable to cover average total _____
and consequently in the long-run would divert resources to other industries.

7.17

Thus, no long-run _____ curve exists for prices below P_2, and,
because resource costs do not rise as more firms enter the industry, the market

long-run _____ curve is a horizontal line at the price P_2.

7.18

Remember the assumption we have made, however, to arrive at such a long-run
industry supply curve. We have assumed that an increase in demand for factor
inputs resulting from an increase in production would not cause any increase in
their prices, and consequently, there would be no resulting increase in the

_____ curves of the firms in the industry.

7.19

How realistic this assumption is may depend on the size of the industry. Most
industries compete in the same markets for factor inputs. The automobile
industry, the ship-building industry, the consumers' durables industries, and
many more all compete, for instance, for steel just as they all compete for labor
and many more factor inputs. Now, if an industry is very small relative to all
others competing for those factor inputs, a small increase in its demand for,
let us say, steel may have a negligible influence on the market price of steel;
and thus, as far as steel is concerned, this industry could expand without

causing an _____ in the cost of steel to itself or to the other industries using steel as a factor input.

Answers

15. $0q_1$ · $0Q_{75}$
16. cost
17. supply · supply
18. cost
19. increase

7.20

Thus, if one industry is small and is only one of many using certain factor inputs,

the _(more/less)___ likely it will be to have an influence on the _____
of any factor input, and, thus, the more _(elastic/inelastic)___ will be this industry's
long-run supply curve. In the limiting case where the industry can expand without increasing the price of any factor input, the long-run supply curve will be

completely _____ .

7.21

For most industries, however, if we assume that additional factor inputs are forth-

coming only at higher prices, the long-run industry _____ curve

will not be a _____ line, but will be upward sloping.

7.22

Consider Figure 7.5. In this instance, as firms move into the industry in their

search for _____ , the increased demand for factor inputs causes
their price to rise. (We shall see precisely how prices are determined in the next
chapter.)

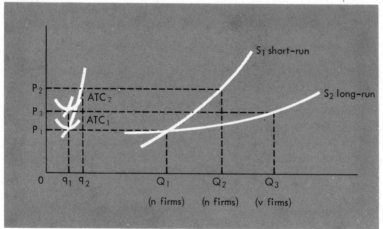

FIGURE 7.5   Long-run supply (increasing cost)

Answers

20.   less · price · elastic · elastic (horizontal)
21.   supply · horizontal
22.   profits

7.23

As factor prices increase, the cost of producing a unit of output would

_____ , and, consequently, the average total cost curve of each firm would shift up.

7.24

Originally at a price of P_1, the firm depicted in Figure 7.5 was producing output _____ . There were n firms in the market, and the total quantity supplied was _____ .

7.25

If the price rose to P_2, marginal revenue would, of course, increase from P_1 to P_2. Each firm would _____ its output to the point at which marginal revenue equalled marginal _____ , that is, each firm would increase output to _____ .

7.26

There would still be only n firms in the short-run, but each would be earning a profit because price or average revenue would be greater than _____

_____ _____ .

7.27

Profit would attract new firms. If such entry caused factor prices to rise, we can depict the rise in costs by shifting _(upwards/downwards)_ the average total cost curve.

7.28

Looking at Figure 7.5, we can see the shift of ATC_1 to ATC_2. With this rise, a price of _____ is required to cover average total costs.

Answers

23. increase
24. $0q_1$ · $0Q_1$
25. increase · cost · $0q_2$
26. average total cost
27. upwards
28. P_3

7.29

Thus, with only n firms in the market, market supply equaled _____ at a price of P_1. Each firm was covering its average total costs.

7.30

With a larger market supply in the long-run, we now have more firms (v firms),

and although each, if identical, is supplying _____ , average

total costs have risen. It therefore requires a _____ price to cover the higher costs. Thus, in the long-run, because a greater supply is forthcoming,

only at a higher price will the long-run supply curve be _____ sloping.

7.31

It could be possible, of course, to have a situation in which an increase in demand for factors of production would lead to a decrease in their prices. If this did happen, the firm's average total cost curve would _(rise/fall)_ , and the long-run supply curve of the industry would be _(positively/negatively)_ inclined. Because this is the unlikely situation, we can ignore it.

REVIEW QUESTIONS

Questions 1 and 2 are based on the following information.

In an economy where there is unrestricted competition in all markets, coal is the primary source of heat for most households. Suppose a supply of natural gas that can provide heat at a much lower cost is discovered.

7.1

Assuming the cost per ton of coal changes in the same direction as industry output, what effect will the discovery have on the price of coal and the quantity of coal produced?

a. price will increase; quantity will decrease
b. price will decrease; quantity will decrease

Answers

29. $0Q_1$
30. $0q_1$ · higher · upward
31. fall · negatively

c. price will decrease; quantity will increase
d. price will increase; quantity will increase

7.2
Which of the following statements is correct?

a. The supply curve in the gas industry is positively inclined.
b. The supply curve in the gas industry is negatively inclined.
c. The supply curve in the coal industry is positively inclined.
d. The supply curve in the coal industry is negatively inclined.

As consumers switch from coal heating to gas heating, the demand for coal will decline, that is, at any given price the quantity demanded will be smaller than before. Because costs increase as industry output increases in the coal industry, that is, the supply curve is positively inclined, the gas discovery will lead to a lower price and a smaller output in the coal industry. We are given no information on costs in the gas industry. The correct response to 7.1 is b and to 7.2 is c.

7.3
If a competitive industry were in long-run equilibrium, which of the following would be correct?

1. Price would equal firm short-run marginal cost.
2. Price would equal firm long-run marginal cost.
3. The industry supply curve would be a horizontal line.
    a. 1 only
    b. 2 only
    c. 1 and 2 only
    d. 1, 2, and 3

In industry, equilibrium in a competitive industry price must equal both a firm's long-run and short-run marginal cost. This says nothing, however, about the shape of the long-run industry supply curve, which could be horizontal, or positively or negatively inclined. The correct response is c.

7.4
If an increase in the demand for aircraft causes the price of aluminum to rise, how will this, other things unchanged, affect the aluminum can industry? (Although it is not true, assume there is only one quality of aluminum.)

a. Output of the aluminum can industry will increase.
b. The long-run supply curve of the aluminum can industry will shift to the right.
c. The long-run supply curve of the aluminum can industry will shift to the left.
d. The long-run supply curve of the aluminum can industry will be unaffected.

As the price of aluminum rises, the cost curves of the aluminum can industry will shift up; that is, aluminum cans will be more expensive to produce. In the long-run, therefore, to cover costs the price of aluminum cans must rise; that is, the same quantity will be forthcoming only at a higher price. The long-run supply curve will shift upwards or to the left. The correct response is c.

8

Price Determination and Market Equilibrium

8.1

Let us see how the price and quantity of a commodity are determined in the market by the interaction of the industry demand and supply curves. We can begin with the short-run equilibrium position of the industry. Consider now Table 8.1. The first two columns, if plotted, would give a normally shaped

_____ curve for sweat shirts. This _____ curve would slope _____ from left to right. The position of this curve would be determined by a set of _____ , the independent variable being _____ , and the dependent variable being _____ .

8.2

If each sweat shirt were priced at $7, the quantity that would be demanded at this price would be _____ . If the price of sweat shirts were to change to $6 per unit, the demand curve represented by the first and second columns would shift. *(yes/no)*____

Answers

1. demand · demand · downwards · parameters · price · quantity
2. 60 · no

Table 8.1

DEMAND AND SUPPLY SCHEDULES OF SWEAT SHIRTS

Price per sweat shirt	Quantity that would be demanded	Quantity that would be supplied
1	180	0
2	160	40
3	140	80
4	120	120
5	100	160
6	80	200
7	60	240
8	40	280
9	20	320
10	0	360

8.3

The figures in the first and second columns are for a time period of a given length, say one week. If we were to draw the demand curve for a time period of five weeks, it would be to the ___(left/right)___ of the demand curve for a time period of one week.

8.4

In a similar fashion, if we were to draw a curve for the first and third columns in Table 8.1, we would have a _____ curve that would slope up-wards from _____ to _____ . This curve would be similar to our demand curve in the sense that its position would be determined by a set of _____ . The dependent variable would again be _____ , and the independent variable _____ .

8.5

Imagine that all potential buyers of your college's sweat shirts get together with all the potential suppliers of sweat shirts, and they hire an auctioneer. Imagine that the auctioneer starts with a price of $3, saying to the potential buyers, "How many sweat shirts would you buy at a price of $3?" The

Answers

    3. right
    4. supply · left · right · parameters · quantity · price

potential consumers will answer _____ . Then, the auctioneer
asks the suppliers, "How many sweat shirts would you be willing to supply at

$3?" The potential suppliers will answer _____ . The auctioneer
will see that at a price of $3 the quantity that would be demanded is

_____ than the quantity that would be supplied.

8.6
Because it is the purpose of the auctioneer to achieve an equilibrium solution,
that is, to have no unsatisfied buyers or sellers, $3 cannot be the equilibrium
price. As long as the quantity that would be supplied is less than the quantity
that would be demanded, some consumers would not be in _____ ,
because they would be willing to buy the good at the market price but would
be unable to find any of the good left for sale. In order to reach an equilibrium,

the auctioneer must change the _____ .

8.7
The auctioneer has taken a course in economics and knows about normally
shaped demand and supply curves. He knows that if he chooses a higher

price, the quantity that would be demanded will be _____ ,

and the quantity that would be supplied will be _____ than the
corresponding quantities at a price of $3.

8.8
Suppose the next price he chooses is $6 per unit. Again, he asks the potential
buyers how many sweat shirts they would buy at a price of $6, and they

reply _____ . And the potential suppliers tell him they would

supply _____ sweat shirts at a price of $6.

8.9
He sees that at a price of $6 the quantity that would be demanded is _____
than the quantity that would be supplied. At a price of $3, we would have

Answers

5. 140 · 80 · greater
6. equilibrium · price
7. less · greater
8. 80 · 200
9. less

excess demand (the quantity that would be demanded is in excess of the quantity that would be supplied), and, as you might expect, at a price of $6,

we would have a situation of excess _____ .

8.10
It is only at a price of $ _____ per unit that the quantity that would be demanded is equal to the quantity that would be supplied in that time period. Thus, we would say that in the market under consideration a price of_____

per unit of good X is the equilibrium price, and a quantity of _____ is the equilibrium quantity.

8.11
This price is known as the equilibrium price because once this price has been established in this market there will, *ceteris paribus,* be no tendency for the price to move from $4 because at this price the quantity that would be demand-

ed just _____ the quantity that would be supplied.

8.12
We saw that at a price of $3 in this market we had excess _____ and

at the price of $6 we had excess _____ . But, at a price of $4 both

excess _____ and excess _____ are zero. Thus, at a price of $4, the market is just cleared. The quantity that would be demanded equals the quantity that would be supplied. Excess demand and excess supply are both zero, and consequently $4 is the _____ price.

8.13
In Figure 8.1, we have drawn the demand curve and supply curve from the data in Table 8.1. As you can observe, those curves intersect at a price of

$ _____ and at a quantity of _____ .

Answers

    9. supply
  10. 4 · 4 · 120
  11. equals
  12. demand · supply · demand · supply · equilibrium
  13. 4 · 120

8.14

We can observe in Figure 8.1 what we saw in Table 8.1. At a price of $3, the

quantity that would be demanded is _____ , and the quantity that

would be supplied is _____ . The difference of 60 is a measure of

excess _____ at a price of $3 per unit.

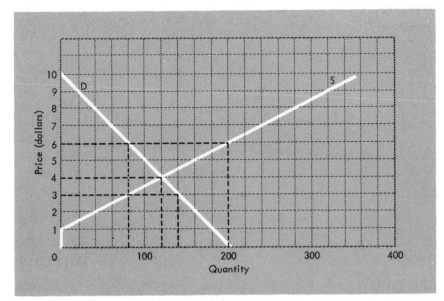

FIGURE 8.1 Demand and supply curves

8.15

Similarly, at a price of $6 per unit, the quantity that would be demanded is

_____ , and the quantity that would be supplied is _____ .

The difference of 120 is a measure of excess _____ at this price.
At a price of $4 per unit, and only at this price, is the quantity that would be

demanded _____ to the quantity that would be supplied, and,

consequently, excess supply and excess demand both equal _____ .
Given the shape of the demand and supply curves in Figure 8.1, is it possible

for any price other than $4 per unit to be an equilibrium price? _____

Answers

14. 140 · 80 · demand
15. 80 · 200 · supply · equal · zero · no

Given that the demand and supply curves remain in the same position as they are in Figure 8.1 for several time periods, would the equilibrium price change?

_____

8.16
Thus, $4 would remain the _____ price, and 120 units would remain

the _____ quantity, because there would be no economic forces at work tending to change either that price or quantity.

8.17
Before the equilibrium price of $4 was reached, buyers were competing against each other, tending to drive price upwards, and sellers or suppliers were competing against other suppliers in an attempt to sell their goods, tending to

drive _____ downwards. This is the competitive higgling of a free

market. Only when _____ has been reached have opposing forces

canceled each other out; those forces determine equilibrium _____

and _____.

8.18
In the real world, there are factors existing in markets that may prevent ideal market situations from occurring. Although an equilibrium price may never be established or, if established, may never remain at equilibrium long, the market mechanism we have just analyzed describes what happens in many markets in the United States. That is, in the free market situation, price tends

toward the _____ level.

8.19
We must now investigate what happens when we relax our *ceteris paribus* assumptions, or in other words, what happens when other things do not remain equal in our market. Let us return to our example in Table 8.1 and Figure 8.1. Let us imagine that the number of potential buyers in this market increases, and this causes the quantity that would be demanded in time period to double

Answers

    15.   no
    16.   equilibrium · equilibrium
    17.   price · equilibrium · price · output
    18.   equilibrium

at every price. Thus, in Table 8.2, at a price of $1 per sweat shirt, the new quantity that would be demanded will be 360 and at the price of $3 per unit, the new quantity that would be demanded will be _____.

Table 8.2

SHIFT IN DEMAND

Price per sweat shirt	Original quantity that would be demanded	New quantity that would be demanded	Quantity that would be supplied
1	180	360	0
2	160	320	40
3	140	280	80
4	120	240	120
5	100	200	160
6	80	160	200
7	60	120	240
8	40	80	280
9	20	40	320
10	0	0	360

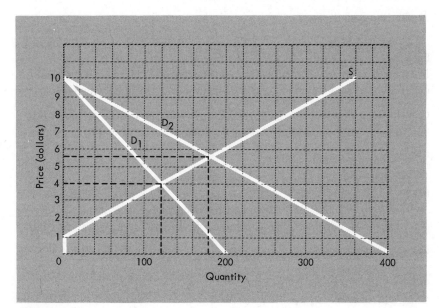

FIGURE 8.2   Shift in demand

Answers

19.   280

8.20

What has happended in this example is that one of the _____
determining the position of the demand curve has changed, and this has
caused us to have a new demand curve for sweat shirts. Let us represent the
old and the new market situations in Figure 8.2.

8.21

We can see from Figure 8.2 that the intersection of D_1 and S occurs at a

price of $ _____ per sweat shirt and at a quantity of _____
sweat shirts.

8.22

Let us now consider the shift of the demand curve. We have a shift of the

demand curve because one of the _____ determining the position
of the demand curve has changed. (In this case, it is the number of consumers.)

If we observe where D_2 intersects S, we shall discover what the new_____
price and quantity are. In this example, the new equilibrium price lies between

$ _____ and $ _____ per sweat shirt, and the new

equilibrium quantity is _____ sweat shirts.

8.23

In Figure 8.2, the demand curve shifts upwards and to the right. When this
occurs, we say we have an increase in demand. Thus, an increase in demand

occurs when (a) one of the _____ determining the position of a
demand curve changes, and (b) this change causes the demand curve to move to

the _____ .

8.24

As you might expect, a decrease in demand occurs when one of the _____
determining the position of the demand curve changes in such a way that the

demand curve moves to the _____ . (Remember Chapter 4.)

Answers

   20. parameters
   21. 4 · 120
   22. parameters · equilibrium · 5 · 6 · 180
   23. parameters · right
   24. parameters · left

8.25

Thus, when we speak of an increase or a decrease in demand, we are talking of

a _____ of the demand curve. This has to be carefully distinguished from a movement along a demand curve.

8.26

When we have a movement along a demand curve, none of the parameters determining the position of the demand curve change, but we are considering

the hypothetical situation of the different _____ of a good that

_____ be demanded at various prices.

8.27

It is important that you distinguish between movements along and movements of a demand or a supply curve. Failure to do so can cause analytical errors in economics. If the market depicted in Figure 8.2 by D_2 and S were in equilibrium, which of the following would cause:

   a. a movement along the demand curve,
   b. an increase in the demand curve,
   c. a decrease in the demand curve?

1. An increase in the incomes of consumers who normally purchase good X:

_____

2. A decrease in price of a competitive product: _____
3. An increase in the price of a complementary product caused by a leftward

shift of the supply curve for that product: _____

4. An increase in the price of a complementary product caused by an increase

in the demand for that product: _____

5. A shift of S down and to the right: _____
6. A decision by the suppliers of good X to offer smaller quantities of good X

at each price: _____

7. The discovery that consumption of good X is detrimental to health:

_____

Answers

   25. shift
   26. quantities · would
   27. b · c · c · b · a · a · c

8. Given that we have very competitive sellers supplying good X, a technological breakthrough that makes the production of good X much cheaper than it

was previously: _____

8.28

Let us now consider some rather special cases in demand and supply analysis on which you can bring your knowledge of elasticity to bear. Consider a street in a residential area where there are no vacant plots. Thus, the supply of houses on this street __(is/is not)__ fixed, and, consequently, the supply

curve of houses for this street would be represented on a figure by a _____ line, which would have the property of being completely __(elastic/inelastic__ ; that is, quantity supplied would not be responsive to price changes.

8.29

If each house on this street were identical, then the _____ price of houses on this street would be determined by where the demand curve for houses on this street intersected the supply curve. Let us imagine the equilibrium price to be $50,000 per house.

8.30

If there is now an increase in demand for houses on this street, the demand

curve will shift to the _____ , the equilibrium price will _____ ,

but the equilibrium quantity will _____ _____ , be-

cause the supply curve is completely _____ .

8.31

When considering most of the goods and services we consume in our daily lives,

we would expect that suppliers would be willing to supply _____ of a good at higher prices. But many examples exist in the real world in which an increase in supply will not be forthcoming no matter what the price offered. We have examples of the number of original Mona Lisa paintings, the number of Rose Bowl tickets, and many more you can think of in which the supply is

Answers

27. a
28. is · vertical · inelastic
29. equilibrium
30. right · increase · remain unchanged · inelastic
31. more

completely _____ . In those cases, an increase in demand in a com-

petitive market will lead to a _____ equilibrium _____ .

8.32

At the other end of the spectrum, we can consider a completely elastic supply,

which would be represented in a figure by a _____ line. We
discussed this case in Chapter 7, when the entry of new firms did not cause

factor prices to rise. The long-run industry _____ curve was a
horizontal line. Given that we start off from an equilibrium position once more,
an increase in demand _(will/will not)_ lead to a higher equilibrium price. What

we would have in this situation would be a larger _____ _____ .

8.33

The supply curves, representing most of the goods we consume in our daily
lives, lie somewhere between the extremes of complete elasticity and complete
inelasticity. Consequently, an increase in demand normally results in a

_____ equilibrium price and a larger _____
quantity.

8.34

You should now be able to see rather easily why it is that some goods that are
very valuable cost so little. If you take a good, such as air, that is very valuable
because without it life could not exist, it should become obvious why we do
not pay for air. The demand curve for air is obviously _(elastic/inelastic)_ ,,

but the supply of air is unlimited at _____ cost.

8.35

Thus, although we might be prepared to pay a very high price for air if we had
to, if we look at the demand for and the supply of air in a figure similar to
the demand and supply figures we have already analyzed, we would have an

_____ demand curve that would intersect a horizontal supply

Answers

31. inelastic · higher · price
32. horizontal · supply · will not · equilibrium quantity
33. higher · equilibrium
34. inelastic · zero
35. inelastic

curve at a price of $ _____ . That is, for all practical intents and purposes, the supply curve for air in the world would be the _(vertical/horizontal)_ axis.

8.36

Goods with this type of supply curve are known as free goods. They are free

goods because the _____ is greater than the amount demanded at a zero price. Traditionally, air has been regarded as a free good. Although air was extremely valuable—without it, we could not survive—it was also extremely cheap. In many cities today, however, there is less clean air than people want, and to provide more is proving to be very expensive.

8.37

Let us now use our knowledge of demand and supply analysis to discover what happens when a central body, such as a government, interferes with this free price system. In Figure 8.3, we have the demand and supply schedules of steak in a local community. Under competitive conditions, the equilibrium

price per pound of steak would be $ _____ , and the equilibrium

quantity would be _____ pounds, per time period under consideration.

8.38

Let us imagine, however, that for some reason the local government decides to fix a price ceiling on the price of steak. Suppose that this price ceiling is $2 per pound. In other words, the legal maximum price that may be charged for steak is $2 per pound. At a price of $2 per pound, however, we can see from

Figure 8.3 that we have a situation of excess _____ because the

quantity that would be demanded at this price is _____ pounds

and the quantity that would be supplied is _____ pounds. Thus,

the amount of excess _____ at $2 per pound is _____ pounds.

Answers

    35.   zero · horizontal
    36.   supply
    37.   3 · 100
    38.   demand · 200 · 80 · demand · 120

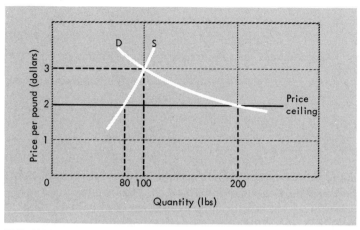

FIGURE 8.3   Price ceiling in the market for steak

8.39
Without a price ceiling existing in this market, and if indeed suppliers of steak had started off by selling steak at $2 per pound, they would have discovered

that this price was _____ the equilibrium price, and, consequently,

price would have _____ to $ _____ per pound.

8.40
At the equilibrium price, the question of who obtains steak is relatively simple. Those people who are prepared to pay $3 per pound for steak will be able to

buy as much steak as they want at that price because $3 is the _____ price.

8.41
However, with a price ceiling of $2 per pound, not all demands will be satisfied,

because the quantity that would be demanded at that price is _____ than the quantity that would be supplied. Thus, we have a situation of excess supply. _____*(true/false)*_____

Answers

   39. below · risen · 3
   40. equilibrium
   41. greater · false

8.42

With a price ceiling of $2 per pound as we have in Figure 8.3, the price mechanism is obviously inadequate in allocating steak among potential buyers, and some other allocating mechanism will have to be sought because there are

only _____ pounds of steak available from suppliers at a price of

$2 per pound to be distributed to buyers who actually want _____ pounds of steak at this price.

8.43

One method would be to have a rationing system in which each household would be limited to a certain quantity of steak. Another way to allocate the 80 pounds of steak would be on a first-come-first-served basis. Or, the suppliers of steak may sell steak to regular customers to the exclusion of

nonregular customers. But, whichever method is adopted, the _____

_____ will not be the allocating mechanism as it is in a freely competitive market situation.

8.44

Consumers and suppliers might also resort to a black market system, which would be an illegal mechanism for circumventing the price ceiling and which

would essentially be resorting to an illegal, but competitive, _____ system.

8.45

The reason that a case such as the one depicted in Figure 8.3 is important is because many countries resort to price ceilings during wars when there are shortages of many basic commodities. Because many of these basic commodities are essential to the survival of families, it is felt unfair that those individuals who cannot pay the high equilibrium prices should be deprived of such commodities. Thus, a price ceiling system is often adopted for many goods, and this, together with a rationing scheme, ensures a distribution of available supplies that seems more equitable to many people. Thus, in situations similar to the one we have in Figure 8.3, price ceiling and rationing schemes can be used in

Answers

    42. 80 · 200
    43. price mechanism
    44. price (market)

situations of excess _____ , and from the point of view of economic analysis, we see that the goods in question will not be allocated completely by a _____ _____ .

8.46

The opposite of a price ceiling is a price floor, and if we look at Figure 8.4, we have a situation of a price floor. If, in the time period under consideration, we were to allow competitive forces to operate in the market depicted in Figure

8.4, the equilibrium price per bushel of wheat would be $ _____ ,

and the equilibrium quantity would be _____ million bushels.

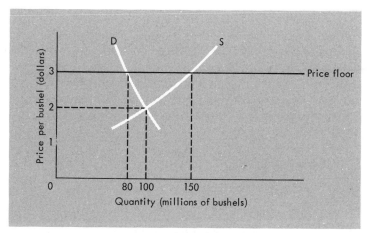

FIGURE 8.4 Price floor in the market for wheat

8.47

However, let us imagine that the government decides, in order to help raise the incomes of farmers, to enforce a price floor of $3 per bushel of wheat. This means that no one may legally sell wheat for less than $3 per bushel, and that no one may legally buy wheat for less than $3 per bushel. With the price floor enforced, the quantity of wheat that will be demanded at this price per

time period will be _____ million bushels, and the quantity that

will be supplied will be _____ million bushels.

Answers

45. demand · price mechanism
46. 2 · 100
47. 80 · 150

8.48

Thus, with a price floor of $3 per bushel, we will have a situation in this market

of _____ _____ to the extent of _____
million bushels of wheat.

8.49

The question now arises, what will happen to the excess supply of wheat? One
solution would be for the government to buy the excess supply of wheat, which

in this case amounts to _____ million bushels per time period, and
give or sell this to other nations.

8.50

Another possible solution would be for the farmers to dispose of, let us imagine
by burning, this excess supply of wheat. Would this action ever be profitable
for the farmers? To answer that question, we must, of course, discover the
revenues and costs involved. What will be the farmers' total revenue in this
market per time period if there are no price floors (remember total revenue is
derived by multiplying price per bushel by number of bushels sold)?

_____ What will be the farmers' total revenue under a price floor

situation as depicted in Figure 8.4? _____

8.51

Thus, we can see total revenue is actually _____ under a situation
of a price floor than it is under competitive conditions.

8.52

In a situation such as that depicted in Figure 8.4, the government may also
restrict the supply of wheat. We can see from the supply schedule in Figure 8.4

that at a price of $3 farmers would be willing to supply _____
million bushels of wheat per time period. What the government might do is

Answers

48. excess supply · 70
49. 70
50. $200 million · $240 million
51. greater
52. 150

require farmers to reduce the amount of wheat they would supply at this price so that the amount of wheat that would be produced would just equal the amount of wheat that would be demanded at that price. It this were to occur in Figure 8.4, the government would require farmers to produce only

_____ million bushels of wheat per time period instead of

_____ million bushels of wheat, which they would normally pro-

duce were the price floor _____ per bushel.

8.53

Now, at a price of $3, we would have farmers producing exactly the amount of

wheat that people would demand at $3 per bushel, that is, _____ million bushels of wheat per time period. Under this type of situation, the farmers are definitely _(better off/worse off)_ than they would be in a freely competitive system because in a freely competitive system total revenue from the

sale of _____ million bushels of wheat would amount to

$ _____ million, whereas under the new system, total revenue

from sales of wheat will amount to $ _____ million per time period

at a production level of _____ million bushels of wheat. Farmers are also definitely _(better off/worse off)_ in this situation because, if we assume that the supply schedule of wheat is normally shaped and reflects cost of production, the total cost of producing 80 million bushels of wheat will be _(less than/greater than)_ the total cost of producing _____ million bushels of wheat per time period, which the farmers would do in the freely competitive situation.

8.54

Using our knowledge of elasticity, we can see why indeed farmers get a larger total revenue at a price of $3 compared with a price of $2 per bushel. It is because the demand curve for wheat in this price range is _(elastic/inelastic)_ , as a 50 percent increase in price leads to _(less than/greater than)_ a 50 percent decrease in quantity that would be demanded.

Answers

   52. 80 · 150 · $3
   53. 80 · better off · 100 · 200 · 240 · 80 · better off ·
        less than · 100
   54. inelastic · less than

8.55

Let us now turn to Figure 8.5 and another example. D and S are the demand and supply schedules of a hypothetical good Y. We see that the demand for this good in the price range in the figure is completely _____ .

The equilibrium price per unit is $ _____ , and the equilibrium quantity is _____ .

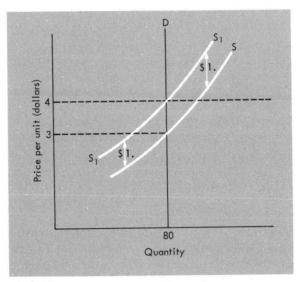

FIGURE 8.5   Tax effect

8.56

Now let us imagine that the government imposes a $1 tax on each unit of the good that the suppliers sell. Before the imposition of this tax, as is shown by

SS, suppliers would be willing to supply _____ units of this good at $3 per unit, but because they now have to pay the government $1 on each unit they sell after the imposition of a tax, they will be willing to

supply _____ units of this good only at a price of $4 per unit as is shown by $S_1 S_1$. We see that the imposition of a tax has caused an upwards

and leftwards shift of the _____ schedule; that is, less will now be produced at each price.

Answers

   55.   inelastic   ·   3   ·   80
   56.   80   ·   80   ·   supply

8.57

Thus, the new effective supply schedule will be $S_1 S_1$. The new equilibrium price

will be $ _____ , and the new equilibrium quantity will be

_____ .

8.58

In the situation before the tax, total revenue, if the market were in equilib-

rium, would amount to $ _____ . After the tax has been im-

posed, total revenue will amount to $ _____ , of which the

supplier will receive $ _____ and the government will receive

$ _____ .

8.59

Now obviously, the suppliers of this good are no worse off than they were

before, as _____ _____ received by the suppliers
has not changed. Thus, the whole burden of the tax has been borne by the
consumers because each individual who now buys a unit of the good is

paying $ _____ instead of $ _____ , as he would
have in the nontax situation.

8.60

In the case depicted in Figure 8.5, therefore, we would say that the incidence
of the tax is completely on the consumers, and, as you might guess, this is

because the demand curve for this good is completely _____ .

8.61

Now consider the case in Figure 8.6. In this situation, we have a completely

_____ demand curve, and in the pretax situation the equilib-

rium price is $ _____ per unit and the equilibrium quantity

Answers

57. 4 · 80
58. 240 · 320 · 240 · 80
59. total revenue · 4 · 3
60. inelastic
61. elastic · 3

_____ . After the tax has been imposed, the equilibrium price is

$ _____ per unit, and the equilibrium quantity is _____ .

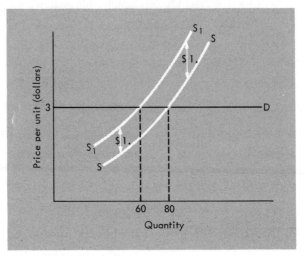

FIGURE 8.6 Tax effect

8.62
Again, we can see that the imposition of a $1 per unit tax has caused the

_____ schedule to shift to the left. Now, had consumers purchased only 60 units of the good in the pretax situation, the total revenue

collected by the suppliers would have been $ _____ . After the
tax has been imposed, however, the equilibrium quantity that will be purchased will actually be 60 units. And in this case, the total revenue will again

be $ _____ , but out of this sum suppliers will have to give

$ _____ to the government. Thus, we see that the total inci-
dence of the tax in this situation is on the _(consumers/suppliers)_ .

8.63
We have chosen extreme examples to show how to determine the incidence
of the tax. You should now work through some examples for yourself with
normally shaped demand and supply curves, bearing in mind that the more
elastic the demand curve is relative to the supply curve, the greater will be

Answers
  61. 80 · 3 · 60
  62. supply · 180 · 180 · 60 · suppliers

the burden of tax borne by the _____ , whereas the more inelastic the demand curve is relative to the supply curve, the greater will be

the burden of the tax borne by the _____ .

8.64
If we return to the world of perfectly competitive markets, we are now in a
position to analyze the importance of the price mechanism in allocating

scarce productive _____ .

8.65
We have assumed throughout that all consumers and firms are competitors. This
means, that when making consumption and production decisions, consumers
and firms act as price takers. That is, they do not consider that their decisions

to buy or produce a good will have any noticeable effect on the _____
of that good in the competitive markets.

8.66
Let us pull together the main ideas and basic economic tools that we have
learned, and show the role of the price mechanism in allocating resources. In
the discussion of demand, we assumed that consumers would spend their

_____ according to their preferences. Formally, we say that consumers allocate their limited income in such a way as to maximize total

_____ . The condition for such a maximum to be attained is that

the _____ utility from the last dollar spent be the same for all
goods and services.

8.67
When the price of a particular good falls, the amount of that good that a dollar
can buy _(increases/decreases)_ . Consequently, when the price of a good falls,
the marginal utility derived from the last dollar spent on a good will
(increase/decrease) . This will encourage consumers to buy more of that good
to meet the marginal equivalency condition necessary for a maximum.

Answers
63. suppliers · consumers
64. resources
65. price
66. income · utility · marginal
67. increases · increase

8.68

Another way to say the same thing is that the demand curve, which shows the quantity that will be demanded at different prices, slopes _(upward/downward)_ from left to right.

8.69

In the discussion of supply, it was assumed that firms try to maximize

_____ . Like a consumer, each perfectly competitive firm is a price taker, not a price maker.

8.70

To the perfectly competitive firm, the going market price for a good, be it a water bed or a sweat shirt, is the price the firm receives for each unit sold or for one additional unit; it equals average _____ and also

_____ _____ .

8.71

In order for a competitive firm to maximize profit, it is necessary to produce

that level of output at which the _____ of the product is equal

to _____ cost.

8.72

The price of a product tells how much will be added to the _(revenue/cost)_ of a competitive firm if an extra unit is produced. The marginal cost tells how

much will be added to _____ if an extra unit of output is pro-duced.

8.73

If price is greater than marginal cost, the production of an extra unit of out-put will add _(more/less)_ to revenue than to cost; that is, profit will _(increase/decrease)_ if an extra unit is produced. If price were less than

Answers

68. downward
69. profit
70. revenue · marginal revenue
71. price · marginal
72. revenue · cost
73. more · increase

marginal cost, it would be possible to add to profit by *(increasing/decreasing)*
output.

8.74
Only at the level of output where price equals marginal cost will _____
be at a maximum.

8.75
This way of expressing the marginal equivalency condition for profit maximization enables us to derive the supply curve for a firm. The supply curve of a firm,

of course, shows the _____ that a firm will be willing to produce at

different _____ .

8.76
A profit-maximizing competitive firm will always expand output to the point

where _____ equals _____ _____ . As a
result, for any particular price, the quantity that will be produced will be

given by the marginal _____ curve. In other words, the marginal
cost curve shows the quantity that a competitive firm will supply at different
prices. That is to say, the marginal cost curve is the competitive firm's

_____ curve.

8.77
The foregoing discussions were put to use to show how, in the market for any

commodity, the equilibrium _____ and _____ of
that commodity would be determined by the forces of supply and demand.

8.78
In any market, unless the quantity that consumers demand equals the quantity
that firms supply, competition among consumers and among firms will lead to

changes in _____ until supply and demand are equal.

Answers
    73. decreasing
    74. profit
    75. quantities · prices
    76. price · marginal cost · cost · supply
    77. price · quantity
    78. price

8.79

The importance of this result can be easily seen. Suppose, for example, that consumers' preferences change so that they consider books to be more satisfying commodities than was previously the case. This would have the

effect of shifting the demand curve for books _____ and to the

_____ .

8.80

At the old price for books, the quantity demanded will now exceed the quantity

supplied, and the price of books will _____ . As the price increases, publishers will be induced to _(move along/shift)_ their supply curve and produce more books. This process will continue until supply and demand are

_____ .

8.81

To take another example, suppose that publishers discover a new, more efficient way to produce books. This will have the effect of shifting down firms' cost curves with the result that they will be prepared to produce more books at each price. This change in technology, then, shifts the supply curve

_____ and to the _____ .

8.82

At the old price, the quantity _____ will be greater than the quan-

tity _____ , and competition among firms will lead to a fall in

_____ .

8.83

As the price of books falls, consumers will respond by _(moving along/shifting)_

their demand curves. This process will continue until _____ and

_____ are equal.

Answers

79. upwards · right
80. increase · move along · equal
81. downward · right
82. supplied · demanded · price
83. moving along · demand · supply

8.84

In both of these examples, we have seen how the utility and profit-maximizing behavior of consumers and competitive firms led to a change in the amount of resources used in the production of a commodity as conditions changed. In the first example, the change in consumers' preferences was reflected in a shift in

the _____ curve. This led to a change in _____ , which signaled firms to increase production.

8.85

In the second example, the change in costs was reflected in a shift in the

_____ curve. This led to a change in _____ , which induced consumers to increase expenditures on the commodity in question.

8.86

In each case, the change in price acted as a signal. In the first case, the rise in

price signaled to _____ that consumers would prefer to consume more books and also made it profitable for firms to produce more books. In

the second case, the fall in price signaled to _____ that books could be produced with fewer resources and enabled them to purchase books at a lower price.

REVIEW QUESTIONS

8.1

When influenza vaccine first became available in the United States, the government set the price equal to the cost of production. At that price, output was insufficient to fill orders, and the government regulated the distribution of the vaccine. Had the vaccine been sold privately without government intervention,

Answers

   84. demand · price
   85. supply · price
   86. firms · consumers

a. the price would have been higher.
b. the price would have been lower.
c. the price would have been the same.
d. whether the price would be higher or lower cannot be determined from the information given.

At the price set by the government, excess demand existed. Thus, the price required to clear the market exceeded the set price. It should be noted that had the vaccine been sold privately at the "equilibrium" price, the problem of vaccine distribution would have been solved differently, that is, having set a price at which excess demand existed, the government then had to decide who was going to receive the vaccine and who, while willing to pay the set price, was going to be excluded. In a competitive market, distribution would have been determined by competition among buyers, with those able and willing to pay receiving the vaccine. The correct response is a.

8.2
Which, if either, of the following statements would be correct when applied to a private enterprise economy?

1. One of the principal effects of competition is to force prices to the lowest level consistent with normal profits.
2. One of the principal functions of profits is to indicate to the government where wages are too low.

a. 1 only
b. 2 only
c. both 1 and 2
d. neither 1 nor 2

Although profits indicate where capital can be most efficiently allocated, they yield no information about the wage level, which in a private enterprise economy is determined by the demand for and supply of labor. Thus, for any given firm, no causal relationship need exist between profit and wage level. In addition, concluding that a wage is "too low" involves making a value judgment. In a private enterprise economy, resources will be allocated in accordance with consumers' wants only if firms' production decisions are responsive to consumers' expenditure decisions. An increase in demand for a good will at first be reflected in higher prices of that good and in higher profits from producing it. Firms will try to take advantage of this higher profitability by producing more of that good, but only if there is competition will firms fully accommodate consumers' preferences by expanding output to the point where consumers' valuation just matches the cost (including normal profit) of production. The correct response is a.

8.3

A city has decided to build 5,000 dwelling units and to lease them to low-income persons at a rental below cost and the going rate in the private market. Other things, such as population, being the same, what effect would you expect this to have on the market for private housing?

a. A decrease in rent, followed later by a decrease in the quantity supplied.
b. A decrease in tenants followed later by an increase in rents.
c. An increase in rents followed later by an increase in the quantity supplied.
d. No effect, because the poor persons who will be eligible for the 5,000 city built dwelling units cannot afford acceptable private housing.

There is a demand for rental housing and a supply of rental housing. The intersection of those schedules yields the equilibrium market output and price. When the 5,000 city dwelling units are complete, the demand curve for private housing will shift to the left as people move into the city dwelling units. In the short run, given that the supply of private housing is fixed, the rental price must therefore fall. This will cause returns in the market to decrease, and, in the long-run, resources to move out; that is, a decrease in the quantity supplied. The correct response is a.

8.4

"If at the going price there is excess demand, competitive firms will shift their supply curves to the right causing prices to rise and quantity to increase until an equilibrium is reached." Which of the following is correct with regard to competitive markets?

a. The above statement is essentially correct in describing how equilibrium is reached.
b. The above statement is correct regarding how suppliers behave, but ignores buyers' reactions.
c. The above statement is incorrect, because the supply curves will not shift.
d. The above statement is incorrect, because it confuses shifting supply curves with shifting demand curves.

Because excess demand exists, at the going prices the market is not in equilibrium. Consequently, the price will rise until demand equals supply or in other words until the excess demand has been eliminated. Neither the demand nor supply curve will shift. The correct response is c.

9

Efficiency of the Market

9.1

What is the economic incentive for people to live under a free enterprise system or under any economic system for that matter? First what does "free" mean? "Free" in the free enterprise system implies the freedom of households to bid for the goods and services they want and freedom of firms to bid for the resources they need to produce those goods and services. People hire out their services, primarily labor services, and with the income they

receive they buy the _____ and _____ they help produce.

9.2

Why are individuals or families not self-sufficient, producing for themselves what they want? In early times, many families were self-sufficient, building their own homes, making their own clothes, and doing their own hunting. It became obvious to such people that they could be _(better off/worse off)_ by doing those things they were best at and exchanging goods with other people who were better at doing other things.

Answers
1. goods · services
2. better off

9.3

To fully understand this principle, let us build on what we know. You have already learned that in any given time period the more of any one good you consume, the smaller the _____ _____ .

9.4

Imagine that living in a primitive society are two individuals who both enjoy nuts and fish. Chips is an excellent fisherman who can, on the average, catch four fish per day, which will spoil if not eaten that day. Coco is an excellent tree climber who can collect six nuts (also perishable) per day. Coco cannot fish; Chips cannot climb trees. Further, suppose that the following figures apply to both Chips and Coco.

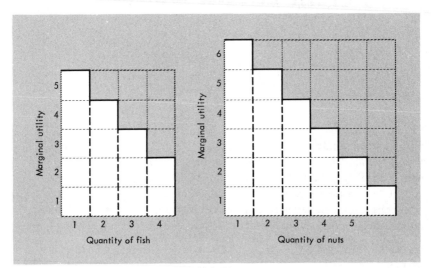

FIGURE 9.1   Marginal utilities of fish and nuts

Both Chips and Coco would prefer, in any given day, a first _____ rather than a first _____ by a ratio of 6/5.

9.5

For the sake of simplicity, assume we can measure satisfaction or utility in terms of utils. From Figure 9.1, we can calculate how many utils Chip re-

Answers

   3. marginal utility
   4. nut · fish

ceives from consuming his four fish. From the first fish, he receives _____

utils, from the second, _____ utils, and so on. From the four fish,

therefore, he receives _____ utils, the area under the "steps."

9.6
How many utils does Coco enjoy in consuming his six nuts? _____
utils.

9.7
Now let Chips and Coco meet. Would Chips be better off giving up one fish

for one coconut? _____ . The marginal cost of giving up a fish is

_____ utils; the marginal benefit of a coconut to Chips is

_____ utils, so, he is _____ utils better off.

9.8
If Chips gains 4 utils, Coco must lose 4 utils. __*(true/false)*__ Not only is

the answer false, but we see that Coco also gains; the _____

_____ of giving up one nut is 1 util, whereas the _____

_____ of obtaining one fish is 5 utils. Thus, Coco gains _____
utils on the exchange.

9.9
If Chips exchanges a second fish for a second nut from Coco, is he better off?

_____ . By how much? _____ utils. By how many

utils is Coco better off? _____ utils.

9.10
Trading would continue until neither Chips nor Coco could become better off.
Although this example is a bit farfetched, the principle is very important. By

Answers
5. 5 · 4 · 14
6. 21
7. yes · 2 · 6 · 4
8. false · marginal cost · marginal benefit · 4
9. yes · 2 · 2

merely exchanging or trading goods, all individuals involved can _____
their total utility. And note that each person is trading benefits without an

_____ in the quantity of goods available.

9.11
Two important lessons emerge from our example. Not only are people better
off after trading without an increase in total output but the opportunity to
trade allows each individual to specialize in producing what he does best, thus
(increasing/decreasing) total utility.

9.12
How much division of labor occurs in a society is limited by the extent of the
market. In some communities, the local doctor provides all the medical atten-

tion. As the market _____ , some doctors specialize in children's
ailments (pediatricians), others in skin diseases (dermatologists), and so on.
As specialization increases, quality and quantity of services also increase,

making society _____ off.

9.13
The opportunity for individuals to specialize in the production of different
goods and exchange them for other goods in free markets will have a substantial impact on the supply and demand for each good. In the preceding
chapter, we analyzed the way in which supply and demand interact and

determine the equilibrium _____ and _____ in the
market for any single commodity. In so doing, we analyzed the basic mechanics
of a market economy. But the solution, or equilibrium, determined in any
single market constitutes only a partial equilibrium because it does not take
into account the interdependence among markets.

9.14
What happens in the market for trucks certainly has an effect on the market
for steel because steel is needed to produce trucks. What happens in the

Answers

10. increase · increase
11. increasing
12. increases · better
13. price · quantity (either order)
14. markets

market for steel certainly has an effect on the market for iron ore because iron ore is needed to produce steel. What happens in the market for iron ore has an effect on the market for trucks because trucks are needed to carry

iron ore. This is just a simple example of what it means to say that _____ are interdependent.

9.15

But although it would be difficult, in fact impossible, to describe the millions of such interdependencies that exist in an economy like the United States', competitive markets, in bringing about a *general equilibrium* of prices and quantities, automatically take these interdependencies into account. It is

possible for competitive _____ to perform this complex task for two reasons.

9.16

First, no single individual or organization has to make all the decisions. Con-

sumers and firms all pursue their own interests and the general _____ solutions is the result of all those individual decisions taken together.

9.17

Second, markets can give out signals that convey to the many individual decision makers the information necessary to plan their expenditure or pro-

duction. These signals are, of course, _____ .

9.18

As individual consumers and firms make their decisions, they affect the

_____ of commodities. In turn, the prices that are signals to consumers and firms will influence their decisions. Changes in prices and in quantities supplied and demanded will occur until equilibrium in all markets

is achieved. We call this solution _____ equilibrium.

Answers
   15. markets
   16. equilibrium
   17. prices
   18. prices · general

9.19

Thus, through individuals pursuing their own ends—utility, in the case of the consumer, and profit, in the case of the entrepreneur—in a competitive

economy, _____ will be allocated according to those ends.

9.20

The decisions of individual consumers and firms, acting freely and independ-

ently, are reflected in prices and outputs in the many competitive _____ that exist in a competitive free enterprise system. Equilibrium is reached in all markets when the combination of commodities demanded is equal to the

combination of commodities supplied, just as _____ is reached in any individual market when the amount of a commodity consumers are willing to buy just equals the amount firms are willing to produce.

9.21

We have not yet seen, however, whether the equilibrium that is reached in a competitive market economy provides an efficient solution to the problem of resource allocation. In the remaining part of this chapter, we will show

under what conditions competitive _____ economy will tend toward an efficient equilibrium.

9.22

What is meant by the term *efficiency?* One kind of efficiency can be called technological efficiency. If a firm, in producing a given output, uses up the

smallest possible quantity of resources, it would be technologically _____. That is, it would incur the least possible cost in producing a given output.

9.23

For an economy as a whole, if a given combination of commodities is pro-duced with the smallest possible cost (quantity of resources), it will be

_____ efficient.

Answers

19. resources
20. markets · equilibrium
21. market
22. efficient
23. technologically

9.24

Will an economy with competitive markets tend to be technologically efficient? Suppose, for example, that some firms in the home construction industry were not efficient in this sense. This would mean that they were using more

_____ to build houses than necessary. As a result, these firms

would be incurring greater costs and earning smaller _____ than would be the case if they were efficient.

9.25

If these firms are trying to maximize profit, it would clearly be in their own

interest to reduce costs by becoming technologically _____ .

9.26

But if, for some reason, these firms did not adopt efficient methods of production, it would be profitable for competing, more efficient firms to

produce and sell houses at a lower _____ and bid away the customers of less efficient firms. The more efficient firms would be able to

sell houses at a lower price and still earn a profit because their _____ are lower.

9.27

The effect of this competitive behavior would be to force inefficient firms to reduce costs or, eventually, to force them out of business. Thus, if self-interest

does not bring about technological efficiency, then the force of _____ will.

9.28

Thus, a competitive market economy will tend to be technologically efficient,

because, for any combination of commodities produced, _____ will force firms to adopt the least-cost methods of production.

Answers

24. resources · profits
25. efficient
26. price · costs
27. competition
28. competition

9.29

But, before an economy can be called economically efficient, it must be more than just technologically efficient. In other words, economic efficiency requires something more than just that the combination of commodities be

produced with the fewest possible _____ .

9.30

It would be possible, for example, for an economy to produce nothing but paperweights and still be technologically efficient. Such an economy would

not be _____ efficient, however, because it clearly would not be producing the best (from the viewpoint of consumers) combination of commodities.

9.31

If it is consumers' wants that should be satisfied, then economic efficiency requires that resources be allocated among the production of different commodities in accordance with consumers' preferences. The paperweight economy would not be efficient, because it would be possible to increase the utility of

consumers by shifting at least some _____ from the production of paperweights to the production of goods such as food and clothing.

9.32

We have seen that a competitive market economy will tend to be _____

efficient. Will it also tend toward _____ efficiency? Let us see.

9.33

Earlier, it was shown that a consumer who spent his income in such a way as

to maximize utility would make the _____ utility from the last dollar spent equal for all goods.

Answers

29. resources
30. economically
31. resources
32. technologically · economic
33. marginal

9.34

For simplicity, consider only two goods, A and B. For the _____ - maximizing consumer, it must be true that

$$\frac{\text{marginal utility of A}}{\text{price of A}} = \frac{\text{marginal utility of B}}{\text{price of B}}$$

9.35

This says, of course, that if A costs twice as much as B, its marginal utility would have to be __(twice/half)__ that of B to make it worthwhile to buy the last unit of A.

9.36

It has also been shown that a profit-maximizing competitive firm will pro-

duce that level of output for which price equals marginal _____ .

For goods A and B, it will be true, in a _____ market economy, that price of A equals marginal cost of A and that price of B equals marginal

cost of B. If we consider together the behavior of _____ -max-

imizing consumers and _____ -maximizing firms in a competitive economy, we can see that there will be a tendency for resources to be allocated efficiently.

9.37

Using symbols, we know in equilibrium that

$$(1) \qquad \frac{MU_A}{P_A} = \frac{MU_B}{P_B}$$

for all consumers.

In words: in equilibrium, the ratio of marginal utility to price for any commodity must be equal to the ratio of marginal utility to price for any other commodity. If, for any consumer, for any two commodities, the ratios were not equal, the consumer would not be in equilibrium; he could increase his satisfaction by re-allocating his expenditure.

Answers

    34. utility
    35. twice
    36. cost · competitive · utility · profit

Again, using symbols, we also know in equilibrium that

(2) $$P_A = MC_A \text{ and } P_B = MC_B$$

for all producers of A and B.

In words: in equilibrium the price of a commodity must equal its marginal cost. Now consider (1) and (2) together.

(1) $$\frac{MU_A}{P_A} = \frac{MU_B}{P_B}$$

(2) $$P_A = MC_A \; ; \; P_B = MC_B$$

Let us replace the prices (P's) in (1) with marginal costs (MC's) from (2).

Thus, in (1) we will replace P_A with _____ and P_B with

_____ .

This gives the result

(3) $$\frac{MU_A}{MC_A} = \frac{MU_B}{MC_B}$$

What does this mean?

9.38
Because MU_A is the utility gained from consumption of the last unit of A, and MC_A is the dollar amount of resources used to produce the last unit of A,

$\dfrac{MU_A}{MC_A}$ is the _____ gained from the last dollar's worth of

_____ in the production of A. Pause here and make sure you understand frame 38.

9.39
Likewise, $\dfrac{MU_B}{MC_B}$ is the _____ gained from the last dollar's

worth of _____ used in the production of B.

9.40
Equation (3), then, says that for each consumer in a competitive economy, the utility gained from the last dollar of resources used in the production of A, that

Answers
37. $MC_A \; \cdot \; MC_B$
38. utility · resources
39. utility · resources

is, $\dfrac{MU_A}{MC_A}$, and the utility gained from the last dollar of resources used in

the production of B, that is, $\dfrac{MU_B}{MC_B}$, are _____ .

9.41

Suppose that this equality does not hold. Suppose, for example, that

$$\frac{MU_A}{MC_A} = \frac{4}{2} \quad \text{and} \quad \frac{MU_B}{MC_B} = \frac{3}{2} .$$

We can show that this is not an equilibrium situation. Suppose that $2 worth of resources were shifted away from the production of B to the production

of A. Because the MC_B is _____ , this will mean one less unit of B. What will be the loss in utility just from this reduction in the amount

of B? _____

9.42

Because the MC_A is also $2, the resouces obtained from industry B, when put

to use in industry A, will produce _____ unit(s) of A. What will

be the gain in utility just from this increase in the amount of A? _____

9.43

Will it be worthwhile in this case for the economy to shift resources from B

to A? *(yes/no)* _____ . Why? Because there will be a net gain in _____
by doing so.

9.44

It will pay to shift resources from one industry to another until

$$\frac{MU_A}{MC_A} = \frac{MU_B}{MC_B}$$

In other words, this is a marginal equivalency condition for efficiency for the economy as a whole. And, as we saw before, a competitive economy will move toward an equilibrium where this condition *(is/is not)* met.

Answers
40. equal
41. 2 · 3
42. 1 · 4
43. yes · utility
44. is

9.45

For this reason, we say that a competitive economy tends to be economically

_____ . When a competitive economy attains equilibrium, there

can be no increases in efficiency by reallocating _____ .

9.46

In other words, a _____ market economy will allocate scarce

_____ among alternative uses in such a way as to satisfy con-

sumers' _____ as fully as possible.

9.47

In the preceding frames, we said that a competitive market economy will
tend to be efficient. By this, we mean two things: first, such an economy
will tend to produce the combination of commodities that is most in

accordance with the preferences of _____ ; second, it will tend
to produce that combination of goods and services with the smallest possible

quantity of _____ .

9.48

In the preceding frame, we used the expressions "tend to be efficient" and
"tend to produce." Why can we not say unequivocally that a competitive
market economy *will* be efficient and *will* produce that combination of
commodities most in accordance with consumers' wishes, using the smallest
possible quantity of resources? There are several reasons. First, the real world
does not stand still. New goods and services are constantly appearing, just
as old ones are disappearing. Thus, for some firms, long-run equilibrium
(might never be/is always) reached.

9.49

Rapidly changing technology—compare the 747 with the piston aircraft or
the containerized vessel with the sailing ship, which incidentally still trans-
ported wheat during this century, or zippers in pants instead of buttons—

Answers

    45. efficient · resources
    46. competitive · resources · wants
    47. consumers · resources
    48. might never be

makes the attainment of long-run equilibrium for many firms well nigh

impossible. Firms, however, still attempt to reach _____-

_____ equilibrium because their goal is _____

maximization.

9.50

Changes in population, changes in consumers' tastes and preferences, and
changes in the relative supplies of different factors of production and
accompanying price changes can force firms to adopt different combinations of factor inputs. Not so many years ago, roads were constructed with
relatively large amounts of labor and little capital goods. Today, the reverse is true. Heavy capital equipment and relatively few men are used,
implying that over time the relative cost of labor to capital in this industry
has _(risen/fallen)_ and firms have economized on the _(more/less)_
expensive factor inputs in an attempt to maximize profit.

9.51

The greater the rate of technological advance, of course, the _____
the output of goods and services available for society, but the faster the rate
of changes taking place in society, the less likely firms and consumers are

to reach _____ - _____ equilibrium. Thus, although
change is something we welcome, it also necessitates caution in making claims
about what actually occurs in a free enterprise system.

9.52

In this chapter, we have seen why a competitive market will tend to be

_____ . This is a very important result that is the ultimate
justification for reliance on market forces in an economy. This "wonderful
world of perfect competition," however, does not include a large amount
of economic activity in our economy (for example, producing national defense and decreasing pollution), and, as we shall see in Chapter 10, there is
a legitimate role for government or collective action on the part of society to
achieve efficiency in allocating resources. We shall also see in Chapter 11 why
some goods are not produced by perfectly competitive firms, for example,
telephone services and automobiles.

Answers

49. long-run · profit
50. risen · more
51. greater · long-run
52. efficient

9.53

Despite exceptions, however, a significant portion of economic activity takes place in our economy as though it were a competitive free enterprise economy . Thus, it is important that you understand how such an economy functions and also be aware of exceptions to general rules. Were there no exceptions, of

course, a competitive _____ _____ system would tend to be efficient by providing the goods and services consumers desired,

using the least amount of scarce _____ .

9.54

Let us briefly summarize how the competitive free enterprise system functions. Consumers allocate their incomes to the goods and services they want most.

In so doing, each consumer attempts to maximize his total _____ .

9.55

Businessmen attempting to maximize _____ produce the goods and services demanded by consumers. Businessmen will produce additional output as long as the revenue from the production of one extra unit is

greater than the _____ of producing that unit.

9.56

More technically, as long as marginal _____ exceeds _____

_____ , more will be added to revenue than to cost, and profit will increase.

9.57

Businessmen compete with each other in resource (land, _____ , and capital) markets and attempt to combine resources (factors of production) in the most efficient manner. Thus, the average cost of each unit

of output will be least when factors are purchased at the minimum _____ and combined as efficiently as possible.

Answers

53. free enterprise · resources
54. utility
55. profit · cost
56. revenue · marginal cost
57. labor · price

9.58

The prices that businessmen pay for those resources will be the incomes received by the owners of the resources. Thus, what are costs to the business-

men are _____ to the resources' owners, who in turn attempt

to maximize _____ by allocating their income on the goods and services they want most.

9.59

In the markets for goods and services, competition will force down the

_____ of each commodity to the minimum average cost of pro-duction. Profit will disappear and only a normal return on investment will remain.

9.60

If in any industry prices move higher than average minimum production cost,

excess _____ will exist, and resources will move into that

industry in search of that excess _____ . This process will con-tinue until excess profit (over and above a normal return) disappears. On the

other hand, if price is below average minimum production _____ ,

resources will move out of that industry in search of _____ elsewhere.

9.61

Thus, in equilibrium in a competitive free enterprise system, businessmen will be producing just as much of each product as consumers are willing to buy at

the price that just covers production cost. The _____ that just covers production cost is the price that is just necessary to command the factors of production needed to produce the amount demanded.

Answers

58. incomes · utility
59. price
60. profit · profit · cost · profit
61. price

9.62

In equilibrium, therefore, the price that consumers must pay for any good
will equal the marginal cost of production. Because in equilibrium this will be
true for all commodities, there would be no way to allocate resources more

_____ .

9.63

Also in equilibrium, as you will recall from Chapter 5, the price a businessman
must pay for a factor of production will equal the value of its marginal pro-

duct. If the value of the marginal product is _____ than the price
paid for the resource, it will add more to revenue than to cost, if the businessman continues to hire additional units of the factor. This will be true for any

factor input until the value of its marginal product equals its _____ .

9.64

Thus, in equilibrium, each factor will be paid a price equal to the value of its

_____ _____ . The income, therefore, that any

resource owner will earn will be determined by the value of the _____

_____ of the resource owned, which in turn will be determined

by the _____ for and _____ of the commodities
that require that resource in the production process.

9.65

In equilibrium, therefore, when the _____ of each resource equals

the value of its _____ _____ , no resource could
earn a higher return by moving to any other field of production.

9.66

We can now see how, in a competitive free enterprise system, scarce

_____ are allocated efficiently through innumerable inter-

Answers
62. efficiently
63. greater · price
64. marginal product · marginal product · demand · supply
65. price · marginal product
66. resources

dependent markets and incomes are paid to resource owners based on the value of their marginal products. In this remarkable system, there is no central control or planning. The actions of utility-seeking consumers and

profit-motivated entrepreneurs lead to a general _____
solution, in which resources will be allocated in the most efficient fashion. Whether or not you like such an economic system may well be influenced by your income, that is, by the value of your marginal product or by how quickly you feel goods and services are distributed through the price system. This is the function of income distribution that we shall study in Chapter 12.

REVIEW QUESTIONS

9.1
In a perfectly competitive free enterprise economy, which of the following statements would be correct?

1. Technological efficiency implies economic efficiency.
2. Economic efficiency implies technological efficiency.
3. For any consumer, marginal utilities will all be equal.
   a. 1 only
   b. 2 only
   c. 1 and 2 only
   d. 1, 2, and 3

Econimic efficiency means not only that goods are being produced at least cost, that is, technological efficiency, but also that the utility of consumers is being maximized. Technological efficiency implies nothing at all about utility maximization. Utility will be maximized for each consumer when

$$\frac{MU_A}{MC_A} = \frac{MU_B}{MC_B} ,$$

and so on, not when

$$MU_A = MU_B.$$

The correct response is b.

9.2
In a perfectly competitive economic system in equilibrium, which of the following will be true?

Answers
   66. equilibrium

a. Incomes will be equal if all men are born with equal ability.
b. Incomes will differ only insofar as people differ in how long or hard they work.
c. Average income could not be increased by labor moving from one firm to another.
d. Average income will be sufficiently high so that no working individual will starve.

If a perfectly competitive economy were in equilibrium, by definition each factor market, including the labor market, would be in equilibrium and each laborer would receive the value of his marginal product. Under these circumstances, total income could not be increased by moving labor from one industry or firm to another. The value of someone's marginal product, and consequently his wage, however, may be so low that even subsistence living will not be possible. Different individuals make different work-leisure decisions. Thus, equal abilities do not produce equal incomes. There are, of course, many other reasons for unequal incomes with equal abilities, that is, inherited wealth. The correct response is c.

9.3
Imagine a perfectly competitive economic system in equilibrium. Then, $\dfrac{MU_A}{MC_A}$ will equal $\dfrac{MU_B}{MC_B}$ will equal $\dfrac{MU_C}{MC_C}$, and so on. Technological advance significantly reduces costs in industry B.

After a time, equilibrium is reestablished in the economy. Which of the following will be true?

a. Prices will have risen in industry B.
b. Prices will have fallen in industry B.
c. Marginal utility will have risen for good B.
d. Total utility will have remained the same.

Due to the technological advance in industry B, costs will fall, and excess profits will appear. Resources will move into industry B from other industries until those excess profits are eliminated. Price, however, will be lower in the new situation because of the cost reduction, and at lower prices consumers will buy more B, reducing the marginal utility of B but increasing total utility. The correct response is b.

9.4

If two individuals were to voluntarily trade with each other, each would become better off for which of the following reasons?

1. Total output would be greater.
2. Total utility would be greater.
3. Costs of production would be lower.
   a. 1 only
   b. 2 only
   c. 3 only
   d. 1, 2, and 3

For two individuals to benefit from trade, neither need total output be greater nor costs of production lower. By each swapping a good that has low marginal utility for him but high marginal utility for his neighbor, an increase in total utility will result. The correct response is b.

10

Externalities and Public Goods

10.1
Although a considerable amount of economic activity takes place in our

economy as though it were a competitive _____ _____
economy, there are areas of economic activity where efficiency would not be
achieved if we were to rely upon market forces.

10.2
Besides studying those areas in this and the next chapter, we shall also
analyze areas in which the government chooses to "interfere" with the working of the competitive economy. The two principal reasons that, as a society,
we choose not to let market forces completely determine the allocation of

scarce _____ are first to help achieve economic efficiency and
second to alter the distribution of goods and services.

10.3
The forces determining the distribution of incomes will be pursued in Chapter
12. You should be aware at this point, however, that when we were analyzing

Answers
1. free enterprise
2. resources

the economic efficiency of a competitive free enterprise system, we took as given the initial distribution of ownership of human and nonhuman resources. That is, the initial distribution ___*(was/was not)*___ questioned. No value judgment was made as to whether such a distribution was fair or just.

10.4
For instance, it is possible to have an _____ allocation of resources in a competitive market system with a very uneven distribution of resources, output, and income. The existence of a population made up of 10 percent millionares and 90 percent paupers ___*(must/does not)*___ necessarily imply that resources are being inefficiently allocated.

10.5
Conversely, we would imagine an economy in which everyone had the same amount of resources and income. Although some people might think that this is an ideal distribution—all men equal in certain respects—would it imply that resources were being efficiently allocated? ___*(yes/no)*___

10.6
For the present, let us return to efficiency, specifically to those areas of economic activity in which competitive market forces would not lead to economic efficiency. Given that such areas exist, we ___*(must modify/leave alone)*___ market forces so that efficiency might be achieved.

10.7
In the preceding chapter, we saw that a competitive market economy will tend to be efficient. By this, we mean two things: first, such an economy will tend to produce the combination of commodities that is most in accord with

the preferences of _____ ; second, it will tend to produce that combination of goods and services with the smallest possible quantity of

_____ .

10.8
Underlying this discussion was an important assumption, which was never stated explicitly. It was assumed that whenever a firm produced a commodity,

Answers

3. was not
4. efficient · does not
5. no
6. must modify
7. consumers · resources

it would have to pay all the costs of production, and in turn would be paid by all consumers who benefited from its product. Knowing the going market price of any good, a profit-maximizing firm, when making its decision about

what to produce, will consider the _____ it has to pay and will

disregard whatever _____ it does not have to pay. It will also base its decision not on how many consumers could be benefited by its product but on how much consumers will _(enjoy/pay for)_ its product.

10.9
As we shall see, when the costs that firms must pay differ from total costs, or when not all consumers have to pay to enjoy the benefits of firms' pro-

ducts, a competitive economy will not tend to allocate _____ efficiently.

10.10
In order to understand why this is true, let us consider two examples, one in

which firms do not have to pay for all the _____ of production of a commodity, and one in which consumers can enjoy the benefit of a

commodity without having to _____ for it.

10.11
Imagine a large power plant that supplies electricity to a city. Suppose that this power plant burns coal to obtain energy to drive its turbines, and that it is located in the middle of the city. What are the costs of producing

electricity? There are the costs of the scarce _____ needed to produce electricity. The firm must pay for the land, labor, and capital it uses

because these resources are _____ .

10.12
There is another cost, however, that this firm does not have to pay. In burning coal, the power plant gives off large quantities of smoke that pollutes the air. As a result, for persons living in this city, health suffers, residences are more

Answers
  8.   costs · costs · pay for
  9.   resources
  10. costs · pay
  11. resources · scarce

difficult to keep clean, and the general tenor of life is less pleasant. Air

pollution, then, is a real _____ of producing electricity that the
firm _(does/does not)_ have to pay.

10.13
In a competitive market economy, nothing exists to force the firm to take
the costs of air pollution into account. As a result, in a competitive market
economy, resources will be allocated as if such costs _(do not exist/are too great)_.
Let us see why, when some costs are not taken into account, the allocation of
resources in a competitive market economy will not be efficient.

10.14
You will remember that a competitive firm will maximize _____
if it produces the level of output for which price equals marginal cost. If the
firm pays only some of the costs of production, it will maximize profit, pro-

ducing the level of output at which _____ equals the _____

_____ paid by the firm.

10.15
If, for example, an air-polluting firm took into account all the costs of producing its output, price would be __(higher/lower)__ and output would be

_____ .

10.16
If consumers spend their income to maximize utility, then, in general equilibrium for a competitive economy, it will be true that the extra utility obtained
from the last dollar paid of production cost of a commodity will be
(the same/different) for all commodities.

10.17
Returning to our example, if we consider for simplicity just two commodities,
electricity (E) and gas (G), it would be true in equilibrium for a competitive

Answers
12.   cost · does not
13.   do not exist
14.   profit · price · marginal cost
15.   higher · lower
16.   the same

economy that

$$\frac{MU_E}{\text{paid } MC_E} = \frac{MU_G}{\text{paid } MC_G} .$$

But we know that, in this example, the costs of producing electricity are

_____ than the costs paid by firms producing electricity. As a
result, in terms of all costs (whether paid by firms or not), it will be true in
equilibrium that

$$\frac{MU_E}{MC_E} \text{ is } \underline{\textit{(less/greater)}} \text{ than } \frac{MU_G}{MC_G}$$

10.18

Because it is a necessary condition for efficiency that the utility gained from
the last dollar of cost be the same for all commodities, we can see from the
preceding frame that a competitive economy _(will/will not)_ be efficient
when some costs are not paid by producers.

10.19

Historically, communities have recognized this problem and have tried to
solve it by modifying the competitive economy in different ways. In terms
of our smoke example, zoning has sometimes been used to require that
plants which make surrounding areas unpleasant to live in be located in
areas distant from residential areas. This approach forces firms to take into
account the costs of air pollution by locating in an area where these costs
are _(high/low)_ .

10.20

An alternative approach that has been used is to require power plants to
use filters and other devices to prevent smoke from pouring out into the air.
In this case, firms are forced to take into account the possible costs of air
pollution by the requirement that they do whatever is necessary to
 (eliminate/create) harmful quantities of smoke.

Answers

17. greater · less
18. will not
19. low
20. eliminate

10.21

Consider another example, the one of industrial firms that dump their wastes into lakes and rivers. Although those firms _(are/are not)___ paying the costs of labor and other resources used, they _(are/are not)___ paying the full costs of the output they are producing.

10.22

The fish that will die and never be consumed, the water that can neither be drunk nor bathed in, the polluted beaches children cannot play upon, and

the general ugliness forced upon society are all _____ that society must pay in addition to the price of the products produced by such firms.

10.23

Again, as in the smoke example, market forces _(do/do not)___ force firms to

consider all the costs of production. Again, therefore, _____ will not be achieved by reliance on market forces.

10.24

Such pollution, or cost, appears in communist and socialist as well as capitalist economies. All economies are becoming increasingly aware of pollution problems, and to differing degrees solutions are being sought. In our economy, policies to fight pollution constitute a kind of interference in the workings of a competitive market economy, but it is an interference directed at situations that a competitive economy _(can/cannot)____ handle efficiently.

10.25

Why does any society tolerate pollution? Why does any society tolerate poverty? Why does every family not have all the goods and services it wants? The answer, of course, to each question is that any society's productive

_____ are limited and more of any one good, by definition,

Answers

21. are · are not
22. costs
23. do not · efficiency
24. cannot
25. resources

means _____ of some other good. If the electricity-producing
firms polluting the atmosphere or the industrial firms polluting rivers and lakes,
in our earlier examples, were to pay all the costs in producing their goods
through other means of waste disposal, production costs of these goods would

be _____ because ___*(more/fewer)*___ resources would be required.
Society would have cleaner air and less water polution but _____
of all other goods and services.

10.26
More pure air and nonpolluted rivers and lakes means _____ resources for other goods and services people want. Just think of the resources
that would be required to make every beach litter-free, including, incidently,
seaweed, rocks, and driftwood that many people consider to be litter.

10.27
Do we really want litter-free beaches if we have to give up schools, hospitals,
horror comics, and switchblade knives to obtain them? The answer, of course,
is that society should allocate its _____ so that the last dollar

spent on each good or service yields the same _____ .

10.28
To summarize briefly, when there are costs of producing a certain commodity
that firms do not have to pay, a competitive market economy will tend to

allocate resources _____ . By having society impose restrictions
that force such firms to take into account all costs of production, it may be
possible to restore the tendency of a market economy toward economic

_____ .

10.29
Let us consider now an example of a *public good*. Here, consumers are able to
enjoy the benefits of a commodity without having to pay for it. Suppose
there is a mosquito swamp that makes life miserable for everyone in the

Answers

25. less · higher · more · less
26. fewer
27. resources · benefit
28. inefficiently · efficiency

neighboring town. It would appear that such a situation would make it profitable, in a competitive market economy, for a firm to produce and sell swamp-clearing services. Because a large number of persons would like to enjoy the benefits of such services, presumably they _(would/would not)_ be willing to pay for them.

10.30

Now, suppose some swamp-clearing firm could perform such services. Would it be able to sell this service? There is no economic reason why any consumer in this town would be willing to pay for this service after the swamp had been cleared, because now it _(would/would not)_ be necessary to pay in order to enjoy a mosquito-free evening. That is, a resident could enjoy (consume) a mosquito-free evening at zero cost.

10.31

Thus, after the service is rendered (after the swamp is cleared), consumers

are able to enjoy the benefits of this service without having to _____ for it.

10.32

Suppose the firm recognizes this problem and decides to have consumers agree to pay before the swamp is cleared. Because in a competitive economy consumers make their expenditures individually, not as a group, our firm would have to deal with consumers _(as a group/individually)_ .

10.33

It is unlikely, even though he might be bothered by mosquitos a great deal, that any one consumer would be willing on his own to hire a firm to clear the swamp. He might say to himself: "It really isn't worth it to me to have the swamp cleared if I have to pay the entire cost. Besides, if any one else decides to have the swamp cleared, I will benefit just as much as if I paid for it myself. What's more, if I were to have the swamp cleared, everyone else would benefit without paying any of the cost." As a result, _(no one/some one)_ is likely to buy the services of the swamp-clearing firm.

Answers

29. would
30. would not
31. pay
32. individually
33. no one

10.34

An enterprising firm might hit upon the idea of selling shares so that no single individual would have to pay the entire cost. Unfortunately, however, if consumers really were to behave independently and in their own interest, they would reason to themselves: "Why should I buy a share? The small amount of my contribution is not going to make any significant difference. If everyone else buys a share, the swamp will be cleared, and I will benefit, whether I buy a share or not. If no one else buys a share, the swamp will not be cleared, even if I were to buy a share." As a result, once again, our firm ___(will/will not)___ find swamp clearing a profitable activity.

10.35

Because there is no way of preventing people who do not pay for the service from consuming it, it is very difficult in a competitive market economy to get anyone to pay for a service like swamp clearing. This is unlike most

commodities. If you want to wear a coat, you must _____ for

your own coat. If you want to drive a car, you must _____ for your own car. But if you want to be free of mosquitos, you can be so just as well if someone else clears the swamp as if you clear the swamp.

10.36

Thus, even though everyone would benefit by having the swamp cleared, it ___(will/will not)___ be cleared in a competitive market economy if no one is willing to pay for it.

10.37

There is a way, however, in which the swamp can be cleared to most people's satisfaction. This solution requires that consumers do not behave independently or competitively. If all consumers got together as a group and agreed that each citizen would be taxed to pay part of the cost of clearing the swamp, it would be possible to pay for the project. But collective or group consumption of this kind is different from the behavior assumed when we talk about

a _____ _____ economy.

Answers

    34. will not
    35. pay · pay
    36. will not
    37. competitive market

10.38

Society has long recognized the need for collective consumption. In fact, one of the principal activities of governments is to make expenditures, on behalf of consumers as a group, for goods that most people want but that will not be produced in a competitive economy. These goods are frequently called

"public goods." Examples of _____ goods are national defense, police and fire protection, scientific research, education, public highways, parks, and recreational areas. For each of these, it is at least partially true that consumers will be free to enjoy them whether or not they pay for them.

10.39

When governments make expenditures, they "interfere" with the workings of a competitive market economy. But when these expenditures are for

_____ goods, they make it possible for goods to be produced that consumers want produced, but that would not be produced in adequate

quantities in a _____ _____ economy.

10.40

In a society such as ours, we elect representatives to form a government. This government, as we have just seen, makes economic decisions designed to

_____ economic welfare. Most of the expenditures made by the government are financed out of taxes paid by individuals and firms.

10.41

In earlier chapters, we studied how individuals spent their incomes on those

goods that yielded the highest _____ . It was an individual or family decision. With government expenditure, however, the decision of who pays for a public good, for example, is sometimes based upon who can afford to pay rather than upon who benefits.

Answers

38. public
39. public · competitive market
40. increase
41. utility

10.42

Consider national defense for example. Suppose we assume that every individual living in the United States benefits equally from national defense. One might argue, then, that such individuals should pay an equal share of the cost. Families with lower incomes in this case would pay _(a larger/an equal/a smaller)_ proportion of their incomes for national defense.

10.43

If families were taxed an equal proportion of their incomes to pay for national defense, the poorer families in dollar terms would pay _(less than/the same/more than)_ families with larger incomes.

10.44

Thus, once the decision has been made to deploy a certain amount of resources for national defense, the question of who pays for this defense will affect the income distribution within the country. The more any one individual is taxed

to pay for any public good, the _____ income he will have available for all other goods and services and the _(worse/better)_ off he will be.

10.45

How much national defense should there be? Society should allocate its resources so that the last dollar spent on national defense yields the same

_____ as the last dollar spent on any other good or service. This rule determines, in principle, how much should be spent on national defense,

but because this good is a _____ good, there is no rule for telling which members of society should pay for it. This decision must be made on grounds such as equity or ability to pay; there is no economic rule to yield an answer.

10.46

Now consider the case of a detergent-producing firm polluting a river. Suppose the community decides that the pollution must stop and that the most tech-

Answers

42. a larger
43. less than
44. less · worse
45. utility · public

nologically efficient way to stop the pollution requires expenditures of $1

million dollars annually, that is, $1 million dollars worth of _____
are required to avoid pollution.

10.47
Who should pay? Before you decide that the detergent-producing firm should
pay, consider the following. Why not have the people who want a nonpolluted
river pay the $1 million per year? After all, if you want an automobile or a

can of beer, it is *(you/your neighbors)* who should pay because it is _____
who receive the benefit from the car or the beer.

10.48
In the river pollution case, no matter who pays, the same amount of

_____ is going to be required, namely $1 million dollars worth.
Thus, the question of who pays is a question of income distribution. Those

who pay will have _____ income to spend on other goods.

10.49
If the detergent-producing firm pays the $1 million dollars to clean up the

river, the cost of producing detergent to the firm will _____ .
Because, in the long run, the price of any product must reflect costs borne by

the firm, the _____ of detergent must rise, and households using

detergent, if they pay the higher price, will have _____ income
to spend on other goods. Consequently, the detergent users will be paying for
cleaning up the river.

10.50
On the other hand, if the local community pays the $1 million out of taxes,
the price of detergents *(will/will not)* rise, and, to the extent that the local
community is composed of detergent and nondetergent users, *(the same/a different)*
distribution of income will result.

Answers
46. resources
47. you · you
48. resources · less
49. rise · price · less
50. will not · a different

10.51

To reinforce the point, consider two people in a room—a smoker and a non-smoker. A widget, costing $1, placed on the end of a cigarette gets rid of the smoke pollution. Who should pay the $1—the smoker causing the pollution or the nonsmoker who wants clean air? No matter who pays, the cost is go-

ing to be $ _____ ; who actually does pay (or partially pays, for example, 50 cents each) affects the income distribution between the two

people, not the amount of _____ required for clean air.

10.52

No one likes pollution as pollution, but getting rid of pollution requires

_____ . The more resources society devotes to lessening pollution,

the _____ resources available for other goods and services.

10.53

If someone else is prepared to pay to get rid of pollution in your community,

you would welcome this because you would become _____ off at no cost to you. But if you or your community must pay the bill, you may decide that the cost is too high.

REVIEW QUESTIONS

Questions 1 and 2 are based on the following information:

Factories in a city with a population of 500,000 cause a serious smog prob-lem. Imagine that the smog could be completely eliminated if 100 new air purification vacuum plants were built. The annual cost of operating the 100 plants would be $400,000.

10.1

Assuming that no single household can afford to pay for the project, but the project's annual benefits to the community as a whole are $600,000, which

Answers
   51. 1 · resources
   52. resources · fewer
   53. better

of the following conditions would be sufficient to prevent a private firm
from making a profit by carrying out the project and selling its services to
residents?

1. Each household acts independently of other households in spending its
   income.
2. When it is to their advantage, households cooperate with one another and
   act as a single buyer.
3. It is impossible to prevent households that do not pay from enjoying smog-
   free air.
   a. 1 only
   b. 2 only
   c. 1 and 3 taken together
   d. 2 and 3 taken together

The nature of the good in question is such that if any household purchases
smog-free air, it will automatically purchase smog-free air for all, and those
households that refuse to pay cannot be excluded from enjoying the smog-
free air. It is impossible for each household to buy its own little piece of clean
atmosphere in the same way it can buy bread. Given this all-or-nothing situation, because no single household can afford to pay the $400,000 annual cost
of the project, as long as households act independently, it will be unprofitable for a private firm to carry out the project. Note that condition 3 by
itself is not sufficient to make the project unprofitable for a private firm,
for as long as households are free to cooperate they might find it to their advantage to make a collective decision to contract with a private firm on
profitable terms. The correct response is c.

10.2
Suppose that, instead of a private firm, the city government were to build
and operate purification plants. The amount of smog left in the atmosphere
will depend on the number of plants in operation. Assuming the government
can calculate the benefit and cost of each plant, how many plants should be
built to achieve the most efficient use of the city's resources?

a. That number at which average benefit minus average cost is maximum.
b. That number at which the benefit minus the cost of the last plant built
   is maximum.
c. That number at which the benefit from an extra plant is zero.
d. That number at which the benefit minus the cost of an extra plant is
   zero.

As long as the gain to society, or to an individual, from producing one extra unit of a commodity exceeds the cost of that unit, society will be better off if the unit is produced. Welfare will be at a maximum when production for each good is continued until the benefit from the last unit produced just equals the cost or, as in this example, until the benefit minus the cost of an extra plant is zero. The correct response is d.

Questions 3 and 4 are based on the following information:

A conflict over the use of the Yat River has arisen between commercial fishermen, who have traditionally caught large quantities of salmon in the river, and a large producer of chemicals, who has discovered that it is possible to dispose of wastes by depositing them in the river. The fishermen claim that the high quantity of wastes being dumped into the river is killing a large number of fish and the chemical producers should be prohibited from using the river as a sewer. No other benefits (for example scenic) are derived from the river.

10.3
This use of the river does not constitute an economical use of resources because

a. the river is better used as a source of fish than as a sewer.
b. although the chemical producer considers the benefits, he does not take into account all the costs of using the river as a sewer.
c. killing the fish is a waste of natural resources.
d. although chemical wastes can be disposed of elsewhere, fish require their natural habitat.

The river is a source of only two benefits—waste disposal and commercial fish. The greater the amount of waste deposited in the river, the greater the number of fish killed and consequently the smaller the commercial fishing catch. Because the benefits and costs to society from both activities—dumping waste and commercial fishing—are not enumerated, we do not know the best mix of these two uses of the river. What we do know is that the chemical producer, in deciding to dump wastes into the river, is considering the private cost of waste disposal, that is, the cost to himself, not the social cost. He ignores the cost his actions impose on the commercial fishermen, and as a result the marginal social benefit from this waste disposal is less than the marginal social cost. This implies that efficiency would be increased if less waste were dumped in the river and more fish were caught, even though it would mean higher-priced chemicals. The correct response is b.

10.4

If the government wants to promote efficient resource use, which of the following policies should it adopt? It should:

a. refuse to intervene.
b. prohibit the chemical producer from dumping wastes into the river.
c. encourage fishermen to fish elsewhere and compensate them for any loss in income.
d. allow the chemical producer to dump wastes into the river but charge him the decrease in value of the river as a fishery.

Because private and social costs differ, as discussed in the answer to 10.3, efficient resource allocation will not result when each individual pursues his own interests. Because the private cost understates the total cost of producing chemicals, the output of the chemical industry will be too large and the output of all other industries too small for efficient resource allocation. The government can promote efficiency by eliminating any difference between private and social costs. It can do this by charging the chemical producer the difference between his private marginal cost and social marginal cost, that is, by charging him the decrease in the value of the river as a fishery. The correct response is d.

11

Imperfect Competition

11.1
In Chapters 1 through 9, we analyzed markets in which competition prevails, that is, markets in which many consumers compete with each other on the demand side and in which many suppliers compete with each other on the supply side. The price of a commodity is determined by the forces of

_____ and _____ . In those competitive markets,

no single buyer or seller has a significant influence on the _____
of the commodity being sold in the market, although each can buy or sell as

much of the commodity as he wishes at that _____ .

11.2
Obviously, in the U.S. economy not all markets are characterized by perfect competition. In the automobile industry, for instance, four companies account for almost all domestic sales, with General Motors producing over 50 percent. Each company can have a substantial effect on the price of automobiles. Thus, the automobile industry in the United States is not a

Answers

    1.   demand · supply · price · price

_____ _____ industry. We shall begin our study of such types of firms with the complete opposite of perfect competition: monopoly.

11.3

Monopoly means one seller. Between the extremes of _____ and perfect competition, we have duopoly (two sellers), oligopoly (a few sellers), and monopolistic competition (a substantial number of sellers but fewer than the number required for perfect competition). We shall return later to the question of whether monopoly is a "good thing" or a "bad thing." For now, we shall merely analyze how price and output are determined in monopolistic situations.

11.4

Suppose the demand schedule for good X is represented by the following data and further suppose that the supplier in the market is a monopolist. If a consumer wishes to purchase some of good X, he must purchase it from

that monopolist. Should the _____ decide not to produce any of good X, there will be none available in this market, as he is the only producer. (We assume that X is a good, such as insulin, for which there is no close substitute.)

Table 11.1

DEMAND SCHEDULE

Price per unit	Quantity that would be demanded
$10	0
9	20
8	40
7	60
6	80
5	100
4	120
3	140
2	160
1	180
0	200

Answers
2. perfectly competitive
3. monopoly
4. monopolist

11.5

From Table 11.1, we can draw a normally shaped _____ curve.
Suppose the profit-maximizing monopolist has access to these data. He will
wish to know how many units of good X he should produce per time period
or how much he should charge for each unit of good X. Now, it is important
to note that, given the market demand schedule, he cannot decide how much
to produce (sell) and also what price to charge. For instance, if he decides to
produce and sell 140 units per time period, the only price that will clear

the market of excess demand or excess supply will be $ _____
per unit. Thus, once he makes either an output or a selling-price decision,
the market, if it is to be cleared, will automatically determine the other for
him.

11.6

Because the monopolist is a profit-maximizing entrepreneur, we must dis-

cover which output and price will yield maximum _____ . For
any given level of output, this will be found by subtracting the total costs
of producing from the total _____ received from selling that
level of output.

Table 11.2

DEMAND AND REVENUE SCHEDULE

(1) Price per unit	(2) Quantity that would be demanded	(3) Total revenue	(4) Average revenue	(5) Marginal revenue
10	0	0	—	
9	20	180	9	9
8	40	320	8 '	7
7	60	420	7	5
6	80	480	6	3
5	100	500	5	1
4	120	480	4	−1
3	140	420	3	−3
2	160	320	2	−5
1	180	180	1	−7
0	200	0	0	−9

Answers

    5. demand · 3
    6. profit · revenue

11.7

In Table 11.2, we have calculated total, average, and marginal revenue from

the data in Table 11.1. Total revenue is found by multiplying each _____
by the quantity that would be demanded at that price. Thus, TR = P X Q.

11.8

Average revenue is _____ _____ divided by
quantity. In symbols,

$$AR = \frac{TR}{Q}.$$

_____ revenue is the extra revenue from the sale of one additional

unit of output. Thus, _____ revenue is the increase in revenue
divided by the increase in output. That is,

$$MR = \frac{\Delta TR}{\Delta Q}.$$

11.9

The data from Table 11.2 have been plotted in Figure 11.1. The average

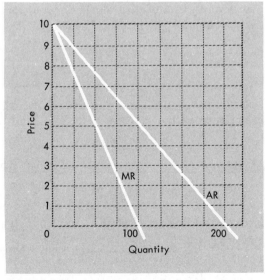

FIGURE 11.1   Average and marginal revenue

Answers

   7. price

   8. total revenue · Marginal · marginal

revenue curve is, of course, the same as the demand curve. We saw in perfect

competition that the _____ curve facing the firm was also the firm's average revenue curve. In the monopoly case, however, the industry demand curve will be the demand curve faced by the monopolist because the monopolist has the only firm in the industry. Thus, the demand curve facing a monopolistic firm _(will/will not)__ be a horizontal line as was the case in the demand curve facing a competitive firm.

11.10
We can also see from Figure 11.1 that marginal revenue no longer equals

_____ revenue as it did in the case of perfectly competitive firms. Thus, for any positive level of output, the monopolist price _(will/__ _will not)__ equal marginal revenue.

11.11
Imagine that the demand (equals _____ _____) curve in Figure 11.1 is for some magic elixir, which comes from only one spring owned by a monopolist. Let us further imagine that the elixir rises from the ground and thus costs nothing to produce. If the monopolist's aim is to maximize profit, how many gallons of elixir should he put up for sale each month? Alternatively, what price per unit should he charge if his aim is profit

maximization? $ _____ .

11.12
Profit, of course, equals total _____ minus total _____ . Because, in this example, production cost is zero, the monopolist's profit will

be the same as _____ _____ . Thus, profit will be a

maximum when _____ _____ is a maximum.

11.13
From Table 11.2, we see that total revenue will be a maximum when the

monopolist charges a price of $ _____ per unit and sells

_____ units. Total profit will equal total _____ will

equal $ _____ .

11.14

In studying competitive firms, we saw that the profit-maximizing level of

output was that output at which marginal revenue equaled _____

_____ . As long as a firm could add more to its revenue than to

its cost by producing an extra unit of output, it would be profitable for the

firm to do so. Thus, firms would produce up to the point at which marginal

_____ equaled _____ cost.

11.15

The same holds true for a monopolist. In our example, however, the marginal

cost of producing an extra unit of elixir is _____ . If the monop-

olist wishes to maximize _____ , he will produce elixir up to the

point at which the extra revenue from the sale of one additional unit of elixir

equals the cost of producing that unit. In the case of zero marginal cost, there-

fore, the monopolist will produce elixir up to the point at which _____

revenue equals zero. From Figure 11.1, we see that marginal revenue is zero at

_____ units of output.

11.16

If the monopolist were to produce beyond this point, marginal revenue would

be _____ than marginal cost because marginal revenue would be

negative and marginal cost would be _____ .

11.17

Thus, by producing beyond this point, although the monopolist adds nothing

to _____ , he actually detracts from total revenue, and

_____ would therefore fall, were he to produce more than 100

units.

Answers

13.   100 · revenue · 500
14.   marginal cost · revenue · marginal
15.   zero · profit · marginal · 100
16.   less · zero
17.   cost · profit

11.18

Most monopolists do not have the fortune of owning a magic elixir spring but
have to pay positive prices for factors of production. Imagine, therefore, that
our monopolist is the sole supplier of an exotic liquor, but that his cost curves
are similar in shape to those of the competitive firms we studied earlier.
Assume, however, that the demand curve for this liquor is the demand curve

in Figure 11.1. This then will be the _____ _____
facing our monopolist.

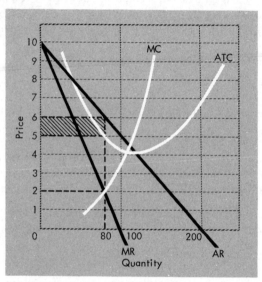

FIGURE 11.2   Monopolistic equilibrium

11.19

In Figure 11.2, we show the revenue and cost curves. If the monopolist wishes

to maximize _____ , he will produce up to that point at which

marginal revenue equals marginal _____ . As long as producing

an extra unit of output adds more to _____ than it does to

_____ , it will be profitable to produce that unit.

Answers
    18.   demand curve
    19.   profit · cost · revenue · cost

11.20

If the production of an additional unit adds more to _____ than

it does to _____ , however, it will not be profitable to produce
that unit. Thus, in Figure 11.2 the profit-maximizing level of output will be

_____ units.

11.21

Once the monopolist has decided what his _____ -maximizing
level of output is, the maximum price he can charge will be determined by the

demand or _____ _____ curve. In Figure 11.2, we

see that this price is $ _____ .

11.22

From the ATC, we see that the average cost of producing one unit of output

at this output level is $ _____ , and thus average _____
per unit is $1. Total profit will, therefore, be average profit × the number of

units of output, or $1 × _____ . Total profit is represented by
the shaded area in Figure 11.2.

11.23

Thus, our monopolist will be in equilibrium, producing an output for which

marginal revenue _____ marginal cost, and he will be making a

_____ over and above a normal return.

11.24

If our monopolist will not allow others to see his secret recipe for his liquor,
or if the government has granted him the sole rights of production, other

firms will not be able to enter this industry seeking the excess _____
that exists. Does the presence of the monopolist therefore lead to an inefficient
allocation of resources in the economy?

Answers

20. cost · revenue · 80
21. profit · average revenue · 6
22. 5 · profit · 80
23. equals · profit
24. profit

11.25

To answer this question, let us see whether the marginal equivalency condition for efficient allocation of resources will be satisfied when there is monopoly. We showed in Chapter 9 that resources would be efficiently allocated only if

$$\frac{MU_A}{MC_A} = \frac{MU_B}{MC_B} = \dots = \frac{MU_N}{MC_N}$$

If this did not hold true, it _____ be possible to make consumers better off by reallocating resources.

11.26

We derived the condition by showing first how consumers would maximize

_____ when

$$\frac{MU_A}{P_A} = \frac{MU_B}{P_B} ,$$

and so on, and second, how, when goods were being produced as efficiently

as possible by competitive firms, the _____ of each good would equal its marginal cost, that is, $P_A = MC_A$, $P_B = MC_B$, and so on. By substituting MC's for price, we arrived at

$$\frac{MU_A}{MC_A} = \frac{MU_B}{MC_B} ,$$

and so on.

11.27

In the monopoly example we have been discussing, from Figure 11.2 we can

see that at the profit-maximizing level of output, marginal cost is $_____,

and the price is $ _____ .

11.28

Thus, price exceeds marginal cost, and the marginal equivalency condition for efficient resources allocation *(does not hold/holds)* because we cannot substitute MC for price in the equivalency equation.

Answers
    25.   would
    26.   utility · price
    27.   2 · 6
    28.   does not hold

11.29

Imagine that the government, on seeing that the marginal equivalency condi-

tion was not met when monopoly existed and consequently that _____
were not being allocated optimally, decided to force each monopoly to produce on the level at which MC equalled demand or average revenue.

11.30

Now consider our monopolist in Figure 11.2. The government order would

mean that his output would _____ and the price that would clear

the market, that is, where MC = AR, would be _____ than before.

11.31

In fact, output would exceed 100 units and the price would fall below $5.

But now price would equal _____ _____ , and

economic efficiency would be established because $\dfrac{MU}{MC}$ for the

monopolistically produced good would equal $\dfrac{MU}{MC}$ for competitively produced goods.

11.32

More resources would now be employed in the monopolist sectors because

output would be larger and consequently _____ _____
would be employed in the competitive sectors. Society would become
(better off/worse off).

11.33

Why, then, does any economy tolerate firms that are not perfectly competitive?
Would welfare and efficiency not be increased if a government forced all firms
to become perfect competitors? Economics would be a very simple subject if
the answers in the previous sentence were always yes. Let us see why the
answers are not necessarily yes. If, as a firm expands, the average cost of pro-

Answers
    29.   resources
    30.   increase · lower
    31.   marginal cost
    32.   fewer resources · better off

ducing a unit of output decreases, the average total cost curve of that firm
will _(rise/fall)_____ as output increases. This must mean that the marginal cost
of production is _(decreasing/less than average cost)_ .

11.34
There are many reasons why such a situation is possible. Each employee can
become highly specialized and very efficient in doing only one job. Assembly
line production and the installation of very expensive equipment, such as
computers, may be profitable if the output level is sufficiently high. Bulk
buying of raw materials may result in a lower per unit cost. For those and

for many other reasons, therefore, it is quite conceivable that average _____
of production can be lower, the higher the level of output.

11.35
Imagine that Figure 11.3 represents the average total cost curves for a firm for
different possible scales of operation. It is quite clear that the minimum average

total _____ of production occurs with ATC_4, at an output level

of _____ .

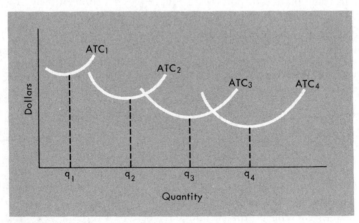

FIGURE 11.3   Economies of scale

11.36
Let us now superimpose on Figure 11.4 the aggregate demand curve for the
commodity whose cost curves appear in the figure. If we insist on this being

Answers
> 33.   fall   ·   less than average cost
> 34.   cost
> 35.   cost   · q_4

a competitive industry, we require a large number of firms. In order to have a large number of competitive firms, we cannot allow any firm to produce more than q_1. Thus, all firms would produce q_1 at minimum cost for that output level, which means that all firms would operate the scale of output given by ATC_1. In "equilibrium," aggregate demand would equal aggregate supply. The equilibrium price would be _____ , and the equilibrium quantity for the industry would be _____ .

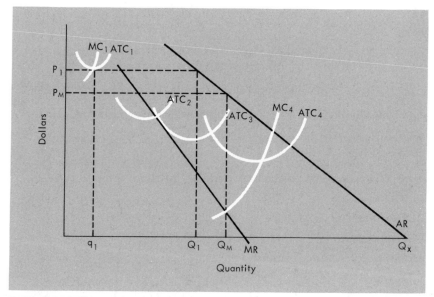

FIGURE 11.4   Monopoly vs. competition

11.37
Each firm would be producing at the minimum point of ATC_1, and, important for our efficiency considerations, marginal cost would equal _____ .

11.38
Consider now the monopoly solution if we have only one firm with ATC_4. The monopolist will maximize _____ by producing up to that output at which marginal revenue equals marginal cost. The equilibrium price will be

_____ and the equilibrium output will be _____ .

Answers
   36. P_1 · Q_1
   37.   price
   38.   profit · P_M · Q_M

11.39

Now, the monopolist is certainly not producing that level of output at which

MC = P but is producing where MC = _____ . Consequently, P
is ___(greater/less)___ than MC. We have just seen, however, that under the
marginal equivalency condition of a competitive price system, resources are

inefficiently allocated when price does not equal _____

_____ .

11.40

Consider, now, the situation in Figure 11.4, when we insisted on many competitive firms rather than a monopoly. It was certainly true that we had

_____ equal to marginal cost, but, in this situation, the "equilib-

rium" price was _____ , and the equilibrium quantity Q_1. In the

monopoly situation, the equilibrium price is _____ , and the

equilibrium quantity is _____ . That is, in this example under
monopoly, price is lower and quantity greater than in the competitive case.

11.41

Consider this case from the viewpoint of consumers. Under monopoly, com-

pared with competition, consumers can enjoy a _____ quantity

at a _____ price. Thus, obviously, in the case where we have
decreasing-cost industries, competition will not lead to optimum resource
allocation, nor will perfect competition prevail.

11.42

If we begin with many competitive firms, each one will realize that average

total _____ can be reduced by expanding the scale of operation.
In Figure 11.4, however, we can see that if each firm expanded to a size
represented by ATC_4, (and if each produced only Q_M ___(less/more)___
than output at the minimum point of ATC_4), the aggregate quantity supplied

would be in excess of the aggregate quantity demanded, which is _____
at a price of zero.

Answers

39. MR · greater · marginal cost
40. price · P_1 · P_M · Q_M
41. larger · lower
42. cost · less · Q_X

11.43

In this example, only one firm would find it profitable to remain in this industry in the long run—that firm that would be allowed to be a _____.

11.44

If you consider the real world, there are many examples of firms that, although not pure monopolists, are certainly far removed from being perfect competitors. The local gas and electricity companies and the telephone company are a few examples. You do not need to be an economist to imagine the inconvenience, inefficiency, and waste of resources that would result if there were thousands of telephone poles and cables side by side on the highways belonging to thousands

of competitive telephone companies. The saving of scarce _____ is obviously large by having only one telephone company.

11.45

It is in society's interest to have large firms in decreasing cost industries.

Because such firms, however, will not equate _____ with

_____ _____ , there may be a legitimate reason for government to regulate prices in those industries. And the government often does so in industries such as public utilities. The telephone company, for instance, must apply to the Federal Communications Commission (FCC)—an agency of the federal government—for permission to change telephone rates. Also, if the FCC considers the telephone company's profits too high, it can force the telephone company, in the public interest, to charge _(lower/higher)_ prices. Thus, if the government can force such firms to produce where price

equals marginal cost, economic _____ can be achieved and the advantages of economies of scale enjoyed.

11.46

So far, we have considered the extremes in types of firms—the perfectly

_____ firm and the _____ firm. In between those extremes lie the majority of the firms we observe daily. They are known as imperfect competitors, and to those firms we now turn.

Answers

    43.   monopolist
    44.   resources
    45.   price · marginal cost · lower · efficiency
    46.   competitive · monopolistic

11.47

One of the assumptions of perfect competition is that suppliers in a given industry produce an identical product. Consequently, consumers _(are/are not)___ indifferent as to whose output they consume. Most consumers, for instance,

are _____ as to which particular farmer's wheat was used to make today's loaf of bread.

11.48

Another assumption is that the number of suppliers is sufficiently _____

so that no single supplier has an appreciable effect on _____ through changing his rate of output.

11.49

If you stop for a moment and consider the commodities you consume daily, you will realize that relatively few meet these "perfect competition" tests. Do you randomly shop for beer or hamburgers or books, or are you like most people and frequent your favorite or most convenient store? If the answer is yes, you obviously _(are/are not)____ indifferent about suppliers, and perfect

_____ is not ruling in those markets.

11.50

If you were an automobile producer, you might be indifferent about which company's steel you purchased, that is, the steel could be identical. But when you realize that relatively few companies produce the bulk of steel in the

United States, you know that the steel industry is not perfectly _____

and that each large company can have a significant effect on the _____ of steel.

11.51

In what way does the presence of imperfectly competitive firms affect efficient resource allocation in our economy? The answer, you might guess,

is that similar to monopoly, equilibrium price does not equal _____

Answers

    47. are · indifferent
    48. large · price
    49. are not · competition
    50. competitive · price
    51. marginal cost

_____ in imperfectly competitive industries, and thus our marginal

_____ condition for efficient resource allocation is violated.

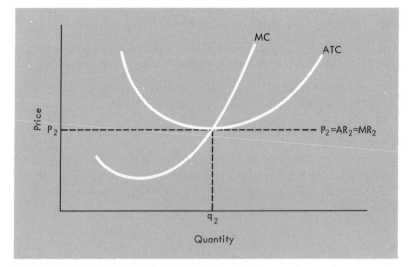

FIGURE 11.5   Perfectly competitive firm in equilibrium

11.52
Figure 11.5 shows a perfectly competitive firm in equilibrium producing out-

put _____ at a price of P_2. We know the firm has no incentive to
change output because q_2 is the equilibrium output—marginal revenue equals

_____ _____ ; any other output would cause a
__(profit/loss)__ .

11.53
The demand curve D facing this firm is a _____ line (at a height

equal to _____ = _____ = _____), and
consequently is completely price __(elastic/inelastic)__ . This means that if the
supplier attempted to charge a price greater than P_2, he would not sell any of
his commodity. All his buyers would switch to a competitor's indistinguish-

able product at a price of _____ .

Answers

51. equivalency
52. q_2 · marginal cost · loss
53. horizontal · P_2 · AR_2 · MR_2 · elastic · P_2

11.54

In imperfect competition, the demand for the product of a firm is not completely price elastic. The more elastic is the demand curve facing a firm, the _____ the response of buyers to a price change. Although the demand curve facing many imperfect competitors is highly price elastic, that

is, a small _____ increase will cause a relatively large decrease in quantity demanded, it is not completely elastic as is the case under perfect

competition, where a small _____ increase causes the firm's sales to fall to zero.

11.55

In imperfect competition, therefore, a firm can raise its _____ and although some consumers may switch to a competitor's output, not all will. Thus, the demand curve facing this firm ___ *(will/will not)* ___ be a horizontal line but will slope _____ from left to right.

11.56

The decision of consumers to switch to a competitor's product will depend upon how close a substitute they consider the competitor's product and how much cheaper it is. Most cigarette smokers have some loyalty to one brand, but, given an increase in the price of only their brand, many smokers would

switch to a close _____ . To the extent that some smokers, however, remained loyal to their brand and paid the higher price, the demand curve

for that brand, although highly _____ , would not be completely so and, consequently, would slope _____ from left to right.

11.57

If the information in frame 56 is correct, we know that the demand for

cigarettes irrespective of brand is elastic. *(true/false)* ___ How do you know?

_____

_____

_____

Answers

54. greater · price · price
55. price · will not · downward
56. substitute · elastic · downward
57. false · We were given information on the elasticity of demand for one brand, not for all cigarettes.

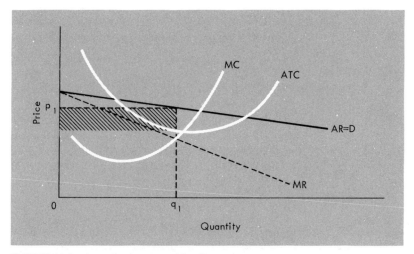

FIGURE 11.6 Imperfectly competitive firm

11.58

Figure 11.6 represents a typical imperfectly competitive firm. This profit-

maximizing firm will produce output _____ at a price P_1 and will make an excess profit (over and above a normal return), represented by the shaded area, that is, average revenue minus average cost at q_1 X number of units of output $0q_1$.

11.59

We know this is an imperfectly competitive firm because _____

_____

11.60

If a situation such as that depicted in Figure 11.6 existed in the short run, what would happen in the long run? Other resources' owners would see

excess _____ being made in this industry and would divert

_____ into it.

Answers

58. $0q_1$
59. the demand curve it faces is not horizontal (perfectly elastic)
60. profit · resources

11.61

To the extent that some buyers switch to the newcomers' products, the demand curve facing the firm in Figure 11.6 will shift to the ___(right/left)___ ,

that is, one of the _____ determining the position of D will have changed.

11.62

Firms will continue to enter this industry until all excess _____ disappears. Figure 11.7 depicts the long-run equilibrium position.

11.63

How do you know that only normal returns are being earned by resources in

Figure 11.7? _____

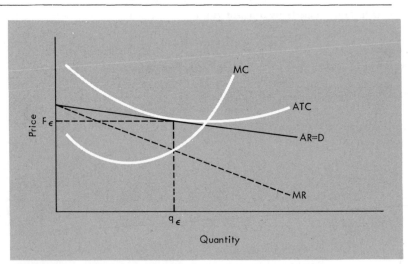

FIGURE 11.7   Imperfectly competitively firm in long-run equilibrium

11.64

How do you know q_E is the equilibrium output of the firm in Figure 11.7?

_____

_____

Answers

    61.   left · parameters

    62.   profit

    63.   At output q_E, ATC = AR; that is, neither profit nor loss is being made.

    64.   At output q_E, MR = MC · Any price other than P_E would involve a loss to the firm.

11.65

Now consider Figure 11.8, in which we have placed a perfectly competitive firm, B, in long-run equilibrium alongside our imperfectly competitive firm A

of Figure 11.7. When firm A is in equilibrium, _____ exceeds MC. In addition, the firm _(is/is not)_____ producing at minimum average cost; unused capacity exists in the firm.

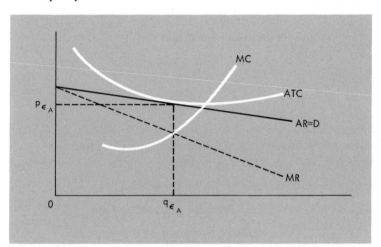

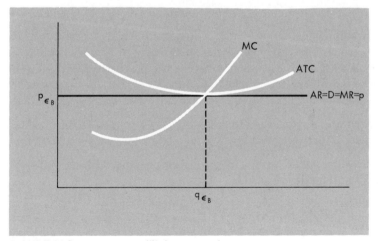

FIGURE 11.8 Long-run equilibria compared

Answers

65. price · is not

11.66
Thus, in comparing A with B, we see that in imperfect competition price is

_____ and output is _____ .

11.67
Because price exceeds MC for firm A, the $\dfrac{MU_A}{MC_A}$ ___(will/will not)___ equal

$\dfrac{MU_B}{MC_B}$, and utility could therefore be increased by diverting resources

towards industry A.

11.68
If, of course, consumers believed that one brand of cigarettes, soup, gasoline, or aspirin were a perfect substitute for another and acted accordingly, and if entry to each industry were free, we could imagine the D curve for firm A

tilting until it was a horizontal line, that is, until we had a _____

_____ firm. Then, MR would equal MC and our _____

_____ condition would be established.

11.69
When no real product differentiation exists, that is, brand X aspirin at 89 cents per fifty tablets is no different from ordinary aspirin at 15 cents per fifty, advertising might convince consumers that the two products are different. This will cause the average price of aspirin to rise not only because the demand curves for individual brands would become downward sloping but also

because advertising would add to the _____ of production. As a consequence, advertising that serves only to create imaginary product differ-

entiation will result in _____ being misallocated and welfare being lower than it otherwise could be.

Answers
    66. higher · lower
    67. will not
    68. perfectly competitive · marginal equivalency
    69. cost · resources

11.70
To the extent that product differentiation is real, that is, soup K is better than soup L, the manufacturers of soup K have some discretionary power—they can

_____ the price and sales will not fall to zero.

11.71
Real or imagined product differentiation gives a downward sloping _____

curve, an intersection of MR with _____ at an output less than

minimum ATC, an equilibrium price greater than _____ , and a ratio of MU to MC ___(greater/less)___ than the corresponding ratio for a perfectly competitive industry.

11.72
As we have shown in the case of monopoly, as long as P = MC, it is always

possible to reallocate _____ so that society is better off, that is, so that at least one person is better off and no one is worse off. This means that as long as such a reallocation can take place, society ___(is/is not)___ using its resources as efficiently as possible.

11.73
As we move from the perfectly competitive firm to the imperfectly competitive firm and towards the monopolist, we encounter the oligopolistic firm that is relatively large in its industry and that has an appreciable effect on

_____ —not as much as the monopolist, but more than the imperfect competitor.

11.74
We could categorize much of our heavy industry in the United States as being oligopolistic (for example, automobiles, steel, aluminum) because a _(small/large)_ number of _(small/large)_ firms produces the bulk of each industry's output.

Answers
70. increase
71. demand · MC · MC · greater
72. resources · is not
73. price
74. small · large

11.75

Again, the demand curve facing an oligopolist is _____ sloping.

Again, a firm will maximize _____ by producing that output at which marginal revenue equals marginal cost. And once again, because price

will exceed _____ _____ , the marginal equivalency condition will not hold, though significant economics of scale may exist.

11.76

Matters would become ever worse if oligopolists formally established a cartel or tacitly cooperated in setting prices. In these cases, the oligopolists would achieve the market power of a *(monopolist/competitive firm)* and the difference

between price and marginal cost would _____ .

11.77

In oligopolistic industries, compared with imperfectly competitive industries, entry by other firms is often extremely expensive, and the existence of excess

or above-normal _____ may not attract resources into this industry. Or other barriers to entry, such as patents, may exclude potential competitors. In an attempt to lessen the power of oligopolists and monopolists, antitrust laws have been passed, beginning with the Sherman Act in 1890. Those laws are not only aimed at limiting the power of oligopolists but also constitute an attempt to achieve more efficient resource allocation.

REVIEW QUESTIONS

11.1

Yoyos are produced by many competing firms. At present levels of production, costs per yoyo would increase if output increased. If a profit maximizing monopolist were to buy out all the present producers, how would the quantity produced compare with output under competitive conditions?

Answers

    75.   downward · profit · marginal cost
    76.   monopolist · increase
    77.   profit

a. The quantity produced by the monopolist would be lower.
b. The quantity produced by the monopolist would be the same.
c. The quantity produced by the monopolist would be higher.
d. The relative quantity that would be produced by the monopolist cannot be determined from the available information.

By buying out all competitive firms, the monopolist would be able to set the price that would yield him maximum profit without fear of any competitor setting a lower price to attract customers and eventually forcing him to decrease his price or lose all his customers. If the monopolist were to continue to produce at the competitively determined quantity of output, he would find that the revenue obtained from the last unit sold would be less than its cost of production. Consequently, in order to maximize profit, the monopolist would reduce output and set a higher price. The correct response is a.

11.2
In an industry in which there are economies of large-scale production, a monopolist is the only firm. The government legislates that the monopoly be broken up and that a number of equal-sized firms replace it. In the new situation:

a. price will be higher, industry output will be higher.
b. price will be lower, industry output will be higher.
c. price will be lower, industry output will be lower.
d. insufficient information exists to determine whether price or quantity will be higher or lower.

Because economies of scale exist, the larger the firm, the lower per unit cost of ourput. Thus, at the limit when only one firm is operating, that is, the monopoly situation, per unit costs will be lower than they would be if several firms were operating. Such cost information, however, does not indicate whether the selling price of output will be higher or lower. The profit maximizing monopolist would product that output for which marginal revenue equaled marginal cost, and although the resulting equilibrium price would yield monopoly profit, the price might still be lower, because of scale economies, than the competitive price. Thus, because two factors, economies of scale and monopoly power, set up forces that pull in opposing directions, insufficient information exists to determine the net changes in price and quantity when the monopoly is broken up. The correct response is d.

11.3

If, for a manufactured commodity, a monopolist were allowed to charge that price that maximized profit, which of the following statements would be correct?

1. The revenue received from the last unit produced would equal the cost of producing that unit.
2. The total revenue (price X quantity) for the monopolist would be maximum.
   a. 1 only
   b. 2 only
   c. both 1 and 2
   d. neither 1 or 2

The monopolist will produce up to the point at which MR = MC, that is, up to the point at which the revenue received from the last unit produced just equals the cost of producing that unit. This will be the profit-maximizing level of output. Total revenue would be a maximum when price X quantity was a maximum, but this would occur when marginal revenue was zero, that is, at a non profit-maximizing level of output assuming MC was not zero. The correct response is a.

11.4

The government has decided to allow two major automobile companies to merge into one. It rejected the advice of a panel of economists who argued that the government should prohibit the merger and apply antitrust laws to restore rigorous competition.

Which of the following arguments would suggest that the government's decision would lead to greater economic efficiency than would the economists' proposal?

a. Larger firms can produce automobiles at lower cost.
b. Competitive firms would attempt to maximize profits.
c. Prices in competitive markets are determined by the forces of supply and demand.
d. If there were many firms, too many different models of automobiles would be produced.

If economies of scale existed in the automobile industry, it would mean that marginal cost was falling as output increased within the firm. To take advantage, therefore, of such scale economies, the merger would be a good thing.

Of course, you might want government regulation over price as in the regulated industries to stop the new automobile company taking advantage of its nonmonopolistic position. The correct response is a.

12

Income Distribution

12.1
In earlier chapters, we learned the meaning of economic efficiency and the conditions under which economic efficiency would be achieved in an economy.

The more efficiently a society's resources are used, the _____ total output and total income.

12.2
In determining how well off individuals or families are in a society, however,

we must consider not only how large total _____ and total

_____ are but also how they are distributed. In this chapter, we shall analyze the forces determining income distribution and the means adopted by governments for changing the market-determined income distribution to a more desirable one.

Answers
1. larger
2. output · income (either order)

12.3

A nation's total annual income divided by its population yields that nation's annual *per capita income*. Per capita income is a rough measure of how well off, on the average, an individual is. This is only an *average* measure, however, and *(takes/does not take)* into account how total income is distributed within a nation.

12.4

By looking at per capita income figures by country, despite lack of detail on distribution, you would see that some individuals have a relatively high income and others a very low income. Average per capita income in the United States, for example, is almost $5,000, whereas in India it is approximately

$100. That is, accepting those figures, the average American has _____ times more income than the average Indian. Such figures do not say that every American citizen has an annual income of $5,000 and every Indian an annual income of $100. *(true/false)*

12.5

Some United States citizens, admittedly only a few, have annual incomes in excess of $1 million, while others have annual incomes of less than $200. Thus, the economic system of the United States *(does/does not)* produce equal incomes for all; in fact, without some redistribution of income on the part of the government, some people would not have sufficient income to subsist.

12.6

Table 12.1 contains income distributions for white, nonwhite, and all families for different years. The income levels are given in 1969 prices to adjust for changes in the price level and to reflect changes in real income. What can be seen from Table 12.1 is that for both whites and nonwhites the

percentage of families in the lower income brackets has _____ over time and the percentages of families and individuals in the upper income

Answers

3. does not take
4. 50 · true
5. does not
6. decreased

Table 12.1

INCOME DISTRIBUTION IN THE UNITED STATES (PERCENTAGE OF FAMILIES)

Income Level (1969 Prices)	1950			1960			1969		
	White	Nonwhite	All	White	Nonwhite	All	White	Nonwhite	All
Under $3,000	21.6	52.4	28.9	14.3	38.4	19.5	8.1	24.0	9.3
$3,000-$4,999	24.4	29.2	29.1	14.3	22.3	18.0	9.6	19.3	10.8
$5,000-$6,999	24.1	11.6	20.6	18.8	15.7	21.6	11.8	17.0	12.3
$7,000-$9,999	17.7	4.0	13.6	25.6	14.4	22.5	21.9	19.5	12.7
$10,000-$14,999	12.1	2.6	7.9	18.3	6.9	13.3	28.0	15.5	26.7
$15,000 and over				8.5	2.2	5.3	20.6	8.3	19.2

brackets has _____ over time. In other words, a larger proportion of U.S. families enjoyed higher incomes in 1969 compared to 1950 or

1960, and a _____ proportion had lower incomes.

12.7

The proportion of nonwhites in lower income brackets, however, has remained substantially higher than the proportion of whites. The *(reverse/same)*
holds true for the upper income brackets.

12.8

Today, there are about 10 million families in the United States who are below
what is often called a poverty level income—around $4,000 per annum for
family of four people. Does this imply that economic efficiency is not being
achieved in the United States? _____*(yes/no)*_____

12.9

Although an economic system may yield an uneven distribution of income and
also be economically efficient, one could imagine the reverse—an economy in
which all incomes were equal but in which resources are not _____
allocated.

12.10

What determines an individual's income and consequently his claim on the
economy's output? As you will recall from Chapter 9, just as the equilibrium

Answers

6. increased · smaller
7. reverse
8. no
9. efficiently

price of a good is determined by the forces of _____ and

_____ , so is the equilibrium price of a factor of production.

12.11
The supplies of Jim Plunketts, Mohammed Alis, and Elizabeth Taylors and the

demands for their services intersect at relatively _____ prices compared to the intersection of the demands for and supplies of babysitters,
street cleaners, and hospital attendants.

12.12
Why does the glamorous movie star earn more than your hard working college

professor? It is all a matter of _____ and _____
determining price.

12.13
The demands for goods and services will determine the demands for the scarce
factors or resources required to produce them. These demands, taken with the

supplies of the various resources, will determine their _____ .

12.14
Thus, the more of any scarce resources you own, the _____ your
income. If you own one of football's few good throwing arms or possess a
deadly knockout punch or a unique singing voice, you will, other things equal,
command a higher price for your particular resources than your less gifted
neighbor.

12.15
You might, of course, also acquire a scarce, highly-priced resource through
training and/or education. Most doctors, dentists, and lawyers earn high incomes

because the _____ for their services will equal the supply only at a
high price.

Answers
10. demand · supply (either order)
11. high
12. demand · supply (either order)
13. prices
14. higher
15. demands

12.16

Just as nature bequeathed Willie Mays with fine baseball skills that put him into

a very _____ income bracket, so some families bequeath their
children with property or part ownership of businesses, both of which are

_____ resources that earn income for their owners.

12.17

In Chapter 5, when we discussed productivity and costs, we analyzed how many
units of a factor input a firm would hire. Figure 12.1 summarizes the analysis
using engineers as an example.

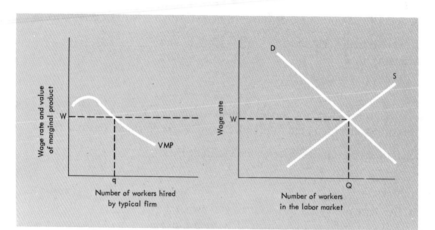

FIGURE 12.1   Market and firm demand for and supply of engineers

In the factor market for engineers, the equilibrium wage rate is $ _____ ,

and at that price for labor the quantity _____ equals the quan-

tity _____ .

12.18

For the firm, we have held constant all other factor inputs and drawn the
marginal value product curve for engineers. This curve tells by how much the

value of _____ will increase if one additional engineer is hired.

Answers

16. high · scarce
17. W · demanded · supplied
18. output

12.19

The firm is a price taker and sees that the going price for an engineer is

$ _____ . How many engineers will the firm hire? _____

12.20

The firm will not hire more than oq because doing so would add more to cost

than it would to _____ ; that is, for each engineer hired beyond oq,

the cost, $ _____ , exceeds the _____ _____ .

12.21

If, in the market for engineers, the supply curve shifts to the right and the

demand curve remains at D, the equilibrium _____ will fall and the

equilibrium output will _____ .

12.22

At the lower price, the firm will hire _(more/less)_____ than oq, but the return to

each engineer (that is, the wage rate) will be _____ than W.

12.23

Thus, in the free enterprise system, the forces of _____ and

_____ will determine the returns to resource owners and

consequently will determine the distribution of _____ .

12.24

What will happen in such a system if an individual possesses no talents or

skills that are marketable? His income will be _____ .

Answers

19. W · oq
20. revenue · W · marginal product
21. price · increase
22. more · less
23. demand · supply · income
24. zero

12.25
Most individuals who earn zero or very low incomes do so because their

potential contribution to a firm, that is, the value of their _____

_____ , is extremely low.

12.26
If an individual's marginal product for a week to some firm is $20, that is, he

increases the value of _____ by $20 if hired, the profit-maximizing

firm will not pay him more than $ _____ .

12.27
At the other extreme, if Jim Plunkett, by joining any football team, could
raise its revenues by $500,000 in a season, and if competition were allowed
to prevail in the National Football League, it would be worthwhile for a club

to pay him up to $500,000, the value of his _____ _____ .

12.28
Thus, although it is stated that all men are born equal, they are _(certainly/_
certainly not) born equal with regard to income potential.

12.29
Those born with superior intellects, unique sporting or entertaining abilities,
wealthy parents, or a great capacity for hard work are, other things equal,

likely to finish up at the upper end of the _____ distribution.
Those born with low intelligence, in ghettos, denied good schooling, or with
no parental encouragement and no inherited wealth are, with some exceptions,

likely to end up at the _____ end of the income distribution.

12.30
The competitive free enterprise system rewards individuals according to their
(needs/ability to produce) , not according to their _(needs/ability to produce)_ .

Answers
25. marginal products
26. output · 20
27. marginal product
28. certainly not
29. income · lower
30. ability to produce · needs

12.31

Should we have such an economic system? The answer to such a question requires value judgments and involves ethics and morals. It ___*(can/cannot)*___ be answered by economic analysis. What economic analysis can do, however, is explain what distributions of income are likely to prevail under different economic systems, without saying which distributions are desirable or undesirable.

12.32

Typically, people in the upper end of the income distribution favor the system, while many at the lower end do not. Part of the reason that this is so is that with a given amount of material income or output, redistributing income in

favor of the poorer people must mean _____ income for those at the upper end of the distribution.

12.33

Although few of the high-income recipients would vote for an equal distribution of income, many favor some type of redistribution so that no family need live below a poverty line. Any such redistribution, of course, means

taking from the "rich" and giving to the _____ . That is, with fixed national income, to make some group better off, some other group is

going to be made _____ _____ .

12.34

Society has long recognized the problem of poverty or unequal income distribution, and many welfare programs that are designed to make the distribution of

_____ more equitable exist here and in other countries.

12.35

Food stamp programs, aid to dependent children, welfare payments, and medicare are programs under which people essentially receive income or payments in excess of their economic contribution to society that is, in excess of

the value of their _____ _____ .

Answers

31. cannot
32. less
33. poor · worse off
34. income
35. marginal products

12.36

The federal and local governments supply many public goods, such as national defense, police and fire protection, education, and so on. Although all families

enjoy to a greater or lesser degree those _____ goods, not all families contribute an equal share of the cost. Of course, the more resources are used

by the public sector (government), the _____ are available for use in the private sector. The more such goods are paid for by the higher income families, however, the ___(less/more)___ unevenly incomes will be distributed.

12.37

The federal income tax structure in the United States is progressive. This means that higher income families, other things equal, pay a higher proportion of

their _____ in taxes than do lower income families. Were all incomes taxed by the same proportion, for example 20 percent, the resulting distribution of after-tax income would be ___(more/less)___ unequal than the progressive system's yield.

12.38

A system under which each family paid the same dollar amount of tax (not the same percentage) would lead to an even ___(more/less)___ unequal distribution of after-tax income.

12.39

Unfortunately, for the lower income groups in our society, not all taxes are

_____ , as is the federal income tax; some are the opposite: regressive.

12.40

Consider, for example, a 5 percent sales tax on a commodity. Independent of your income, you must pay a 5 percent tax for buying the item. If both a high-income and low-income individual spends $1 on the commodity, each is

paying only _____ cents in tax, but this is a _____ proportion of the poor man's income than the rich man's.

Answers

36. public · fewer · less
37. incomes · more
38. more
39. progressive
40. 5 · higher

12.41

In fact, if all taxes in the U.S. were taken into account, it would be found that some of the lower income groups actually pay a higher proportion of their income in taxes than do middle and some upper income groups. That is,

in some ranges, we have a _____ tax system.

12.42

Many proposals for achieving a more equitable income distribution have been suggested. They range from a complete reform of the tax structure to the negative income tax. What is clear in all redistribution schemes of a fixed amount of national income is that to make any one income group better off,

some other income group(s) must become _____ _____.

12.43

Up to now, we have assumed that equilibrium is attained in all markets, including the labor market. But, as you know from reading the newspapers, unemployment is a frequent problem in the United States. This means that __(all/not all)__ workers can always find jobs.

12.44

The type of labor that often bears the brunt of unemployment is the least-skilled and lowest-income earning group. Thus, one way to promote a more

even distribution of _____ is to pursue policies designed to keep

the economy employing all its scarce productive _____ , that is, at full employment.

12.45

By also pursuing policies that retrain unemployed workers for better jobs and by providing better education and training for deprived children, we are implicitly raising skill levels in the labor force. Higher skills, that is higher marginal

_____ , are associated with ___(higher/lower)___ wages. To the extent that the poor benefit disproportionately from such programs, the distribution of income will become ___(more/less)___ unequal.

Answers

41. regressive
42. worse off
43. not all
44. income · resources
45. products · higher · less

12.46

Not all income is payment for labor services. Just as labor earns a return in its market, so do the owners of nonlabor input earn returns according to the value of the _____ _____ of those inputs. For example, the individual who owns and leases property earns a rent that reflects the marginal contribution of that real estate to production.

12.47

In 1971, total income payments to factors of production was $794 billion, of which three-quarters was labor income. The remaining one-quarter took the form of rents, interest, dividends, and proprietor's income. Most of this nonlabor income is distributed to families who are in upper income brackets. Consequently, the distribution of income is made ___(more/less)___ uneven when we add nonlabor income to labor income.

12.48

One reason the poor are poor is that the value of the _____ _____ of their labor is ___(high/low)___ . Another reason is that they own few nonhuman resources.

12.49

Throughout modern industrial history, disagreement over what is a fair division of income between wages and profits payments has been the source of much debate and has had a profound influence on the development of economic institutions. As you might expect, workers have typically felt that ___(wage/profit)___ income should be higher and _____ income lower. Have you ever heard of workers striking for lower wages?

12.50

In an attempt to redress what workers have felt was ___(a fair/an unfair)___ division of returns to factors of production, unions have been formed to strengthen the power of labor in the market place. By representing all workers

Answers

46. marginal products
47. more
48. marginal product · low
49. wage · profit
50. an unfair

in a market, a union may effectively eliminate competition among workers for jobs and force employers to deal with union leaders (representing workers collectively) rather than with workers individually. Thus, one goal of the union may be to provide workers with _(monopoly/competitive)_ power in the market for labor.

12.51

If we imagine successful unionization in what previously had been a competitive labor market (with competition among employers as well as among workers), and if we further suppose that the union negotiates a wage rate above the competitive equilibrium wage rate, then profit-maximizing employers will respond by equating the value of the _____ _____ of labor with the new wage rate. Because for the typical firm there are diminishing returns to any given factor input (that is, there is a downward-sloping marginal product curve for labor), employers will hire _(more/fewer)_ workers than before.

12.52

Note that the establishment by unions of a higher-than-equilibrium wage rate will have an effect that is similar to that of an imposition by government of a higher-than-equilibrium minimum wage rate. Those workers who remain employed will become _(better/worse)_ off, while those who are laid off will become _____ off.

12.53

In certain situations, however, it is possible for unionization to lead to a higher wage rate and no decrease in employment. Those situations occur where there is no effective competition for labor among employers. Lack of competition among buyers is called *monopsony*. This is the counterpart of a lack of competition among sellers, which is called _____ . In these situations, by establishing _____ power for workers, unions can offset the _____ power of employers.

Answers
50. monopoly
51. marginal product · fewer
52. better · worse
53. monopoly · monopoly · monopsony

12.54

An example of monopsony power occurs in the "company town" where one firm provides the bulk of employment opportunities. If such a firm were to try to hire more labor, it would normally have to increase the wage rate to attract workers from other towns, out of retirement, off the farm, and so on. In other words, it does not face the completely __(elastic/inelastic)__ supply

curve of labor facing the competitive firm. The supply curve slopes _____ from left to right.

12.55

The cost to the firm of hiring an additional worker, that is, the _____ cost of hiring labor, would equal the higher wage necessary to attract the new worker plus the increase in wages the firm would have to pay all workers currently employed. (The increase for existing workers would result because the employer would be unable to pay two different wage rates for equal work.) Thus, the marginal cost of hiring labor to the firm is __(greater/less)__ than the wage rate.

12.56

The profit-maximizing monopsonistic firm will hire labor up to the point at which the benefit to the firm of hiring one more worker (that is, the value of

the _____ _____ of labor) is equal to the cost to the

firm of hiring that worker (that is, the _____ _____ of hiring labor). Consequently, the monopsonistic firm will not hire labor up to the point at which the value of the marginal product is equal to the wage rate. (Remember, the marginal cost of hiring labor for the monopsonist is greater than the wage rate.) The wage rate will be __(less/greater)__ than the value of the marginal product of labor. This is what economists mean by *exploitation* of labor. This definition of *exploitation* differs from the Marxian definition.

12.57

When dealing with monopsonist employers, by successfully negotiating a fixed wage rate that is higher than the initial wage rate, a union can actually reduce the marginal cost of hiring labor. At the new fixed wage, the firm can

Answers

    54. elastic · upward
    55. marginal · greater
    56. marginal product · marginal cost · less

hire an additional worker at the negotiated rate and ____*(will/will not)*____ have to pay existing workers higher wages whenever an additional worker is hired. Thus, even though the wage rate is higher, the employer will hire *(more/fewer)* , because the marginal cost of hiring labor is lower.

12.58
In monopsony situations, unionization and collective bargaining shift the supply curve of labor facing the firm so that it becomes a horizontal line instead of an upward sloping line. In other words, the cost to the firm of hiring an additional worker *(rises above/remains constant at)* the negotiated wage up to the point where there are no more people willing to work at that wage.

12.59
Much of the debate over the effectiveness and desirability of unionization centers on the extent to which they decrease employment opportunities by artificially restricting the supply of labor to firms, or alternatively make all workers better off by eliminating exploitation of labor. Put another way, the issue is whether

unions create _____ power for workers or offset _____ power of employers.

REVIEW QUESTIONS

12.1
Is the following statement correct or incorrect and why?

"Economic analysis has shown that to increase economic welfare any policy that would increase economic efficiency should always be undertaken."

a. Correct, because an improved allocation of resources *will* increase every person's real income.
b. Correct, because an improved allocation of resources *can* increase every person's real income.
c. Incorrect, because an improved allocation of resources *can* increase every person's real income, but *may* reduce some person's income.
d. Incorrect, because an improved allocation of resources *cannot* increase every person's real income.

Answers
    57. will not · more
    58. remains constant at
    59. monopoly · monopsony

An increase in economic efficiency, for example, producing more goods than before from the same resources, means it is possible to make some people better off without making anyone worse off. However, an increase in economic efficiency does not guarantee that some people will not suffer. Thus, while improved resource allocation can increase every person's real income, the actual reallocation of resources, for example, introducing cheaper production methods in agriculture and reducing labor requirements, may make some people worse off. To conclude that any increase in efficiency should *always* be undertaken requires a value judgment regarding the distribution of income. Consequently, it is incorrect to say that economic analysis has shown that all changes that increase economic efficiency should be made because economic analysis can only draw positive, not normative, conclusions. The correct response is c.

12.2

Questions 2 and 3 are based on the following information.

For a particular income tax system, the first $900 of income is exempt, and the remainder is taxed at a 90 percent rate.

   How is the ratio of a high income (say $10,000 before tax) to a low income (say $1,000 before tax) affected by the tax system?

a. The after-tax ratio is higher, that is, the system is regressive.
b. The after-tax ratio is lower, that is, the system is progressive.
c. The after-tax ratio is the same, that is, the system is proportional.
d. The after-tax ratio could be higher or lower, depending upon the income level.

For incomes greater than $900, even though the marginal tax rate (the tax rate on the last dollar of income) is constant, it exceeds the average tax rate (total tax divided by total income). Consequently, the average tax rate increases and the system is progressive. For example, an income of $1,000 will be taxed $90, which gives an average tax rate of 9 percent. An income of $10,000 will be taxed $8,190, which gives an average tax rate of 81.0 percent. In this example, the ratio of the two incomes before tax was 10:1 and the ratio after tax was approximately 2:1. A rising average tax rate is consistent with a constant marginal tax rate because the first $900 is exempt from tax. This relationship is similar to that between average cost and marginal cost for a firm with positive fixed cost. The correct response is b.

12.3

Under this tax system, Ritchie, who is paid 50 cents per hour, chooses to work 2,000 hours per year. If the exemption were decreased to $100 and the tax rate on income over $100 were decreased to 10 percent, he would:

a. be no worse off and work no fewer than 2,000 hours.
b. be no worse off and work no more than 2,000 hours.
c. be no better off and work no fewer than 2,000 hours.
d. be no better off and work no more than 2,000 hours.

Under both sets of exemptions and rates ($900 and 90 percent, $100 and 10 percent), Ritchie could earn $1,000 per annum pretax and $910 posttax. Because under the new exemption and rate ($100 and 10 percent) Ritchie can earn as much posttax income as previously by working the same number of hours, he can be no worse off than before, but he may be better off. He will be better off if the after-tax hourly income of 45 cents for an additional hour's work is worth more to him than an extra hour of leisure. By choosing to work only 2,000 hours, initially we know that an extra hour of leisure was worth more than 5 cents—the after-tax return for one extra hour worked. If the 45 cents posttax rate is worth more than an extra hour of leisure, not only will Ritchie be better off, he will work more than 2,000 hours. The correct response is a.

12.4
On which of the following can an economist offer only a personal opinion, not professional analysis?

a. whether farmers' incomes would increase if all price supports were removed
b. whether taxes should be changed to distribute income more evenly
c. whether a decrease in telephone rates would lead to an increased use of telephone facilities
d. whether increased economic efficiency would result if the computer industry were broken up into a large number of small firms

An economist can offer professional analysis on "what would happen if" propositions, but only a personal opinion on what "should" happen. The fact that an economist might be wrong, for instance, in predicting whether economic efficiency would result if the computer industry were broken up is irrelevant. The economist might have insufficient information or an inadequate model for making the correct prediction but neither prohibits professional analysis. What is the "right" distribution of income requires a value judgment and is, therefore, a matter of personal opinion. The correct response is b.